Scoring Goals
in the Dark

CLARE
SHINE

Scoring Goals in the Dark

CLARE SHINE

With Gareth Maher

First published by Pitch Publishing, 2022

Pitch Publishing
9 Donnington Park,
85 Birdham Road,
Chichester,
West Sussex,
PO20 7AJ
www.pitchpublishing.co.uk
info@pitchpublishing.co.uk

ISBN 978 1 80150 117 0

Typesetting and origination by Pitch Publishing
Printed and bound in Great Britain by TJ Books, Padstow

Contents

Foreword
by Katie McCabe

EVERYONE does it, even though we don't mean to, but we all judge a book by its cover. At least initially anyway. We make snap judgements on things and only by turning a few pages do we get to see the true version of something or someone.

That is how I feel about Clare Shine. She is someone who I had heard about long before I ever met her, so that reputation formed part of my first impression of her. Then, as we got to know each other, I realised that there was so much more to her.

That discovery hasn't stopped, because Clare hasn't stopped evolving. I've tried to think of a way to describe the person she has become and the most fitting term is 'brave'. I admire her bravery to be so open with who she is, what she has been through and how her experiences can possibly help others.

My opinion of Clare has come a long way from the messy room-mate and talented team-mate to someone who I'm proud to call one of my best friends. There have been some bumps along the way, as there are in any relationship, and that has challenged us both over the years. We've grown up together and life has been very different for us in many ways. Sometimes I felt like I didn't know her any more as she would keep silent and I wondered if everything was OK.

Having always been an outgoing person who was the life of the dressing room and never afraid to express herself out on the pitch, it was confusing when Clare went quiet but I knew that something was wrong.

Eventually, she confided in me and felt that she could trust me by revealing that she was struggling with her mental health. I helped in whatever way I could but it was Clare who made the necessary changes that have allowed her to become the person she is today.

The first step in that, which I'm really proud of her for taking, was admitting that she needed help. It's very difficult to go through something like that but once she allowed people to help then she was able to show just how strong she is to come through it all. Of course, she has her good days and bad days but I admire her so much for the bravery that she has shown in dealing with her struggles.

The strength that she has shown to come out and raise awareness for mental health has been phenomenal. It can't be easy to have gone through what she has had to and be willing to share the full details of it with the world. I know that her openness helps others because there are so many people who suffer in silence. That is why this book is so important as it smashes through this nonsense that you should not share when you are feeling vulnerable because it might be a burden for others. Clare has taught us all that it's not only OK to speak out, it is imperative.

The other thing that should not get lost here is just how good a footballer Clare is. I remember begging her to join Raheny United and always loving playing with her in Republic of Ireland teams. She is so direct with her running off defenders, her dynamic link-up play and, of course, her finishing in front of goal. That goal against Spain in the UEFA Women's

Under-19 European Championship always sticks in my mind as a favourite memory.

Clare still has a lot to give on the pitch as a player and I hope to make many new memories with her as a team-mate. Away from the pitch, she is getting stronger and more confident in herself and I know that she will use that in a positive way to help others. This book is only the beginning of Clare's story.

Katie McCabe

Republic of Ireland WNT captain

Arsenal footballer

1

Darkest Hour

SATURDAY, 20 October 2018 was the day that I tried to kill myself, for the first time.

For an entire week I had been plotting my death. I decided that it was the right time to bring my misery to an end and stop causing trouble for those I loved most.

Except most plans never work out exactly how you want them to.

Drink has always been something that I have turned to while struggling with my mental health.

Little did I know that it would lead to me being technically classed as an alcoholic before the age of 23. When drinking, I could speak more openly and I was able to express myself in a way that I never could on an average day. I relied on it to find both courage and confidence.

The day started like any other, at least during that period of my life, with a few drinks too many. The Octoberfest in Carrigaline was designed to bring people together and enjoy a few beers, but I opted to use it to drown out everything that I was feeling.

A few hours later, I stirred in the passenger seat of a car as I forced myself to stay awake. My mum was on chauffeur service as she brought me and a few friends into Cork city centre to continue our night out. Mum tried to encourage me to come home, but of course I had more drinking to do.

The first stop was in a bar called Grand Central, where I decided to alter the pace of the evening by snorting some cocaine in the toilet. With the effects of alcohol fading, I needed another boost. Except this one was a little too strong and I floated across the nightclub like an astronaut taking advantage of the lack of gravity in outer space.

A change of venue did little to bring me back down to earth. In fact, I spent most of my time in Cypress Avenue trying to evade the bouncers who were determined to eject the rabble-rouser who was aggressively bumping into people and making more noise than the DJ for the hire.

It didn't take long for them to catch me, usher me towards the main doors and dump me on the pathway as if I was a bag of rubbish that someone else would clean up at some stage. Naturally, I voiced my displeasure at this. If you're going to treat me like a dog then I'm going to bark like one back at you.

Then I started to sober up, at least enough to realise that I was on my own and nobody was coming to get me. Typical, I'd taken it too far again. What was the point in trying to fight back? None of my friends had even noticed I was missing. Or maybe they had decided they'd had enough of my behaviour. So why wait anymore?

I stepped off the pathway into the main road and closed my eyes so I didn't have to see the oncoming car crash into me. I wanted to be squashed like a bug and bring my petty existence to an end. Goodbye world, nice knowing ya!

The driver, however, reacted as quickly as he could and slowed almost to a complete stop. The front of the car still hit me and bowled me over. My bag swung loose and scratched the paintwork on the bonnet as my torso smashed down on to the cold concrete and my neck snapped forward quickly before I curled into a ball, like a hedgehog trying to protect itself. People gathered around and the driver got out to check to see if I was alive, which I was unfortunately. Wanting the ground to swallow me up, I continued to shout the same line, as the tears streamed down my face. I kept repeating, 'I just want to die.'

I had failed in my attempt to commit suicide. I couldn't do anything right, even when it came to killing myself. This was my darkest hour and yet I still came through it, which meant a lot more suffering was to come because I had serious mental health problems and they were not going to disappear anytime soon.

Initially my intention was to slip away via an overdose of tablets. That felt like the best way to do it; painless, no mess. But here I was now in the back of an ambulance crying uncontrollably, having to deal with the mess I had gotten myself into. How am I going to explain this to my family? How do I explain to them that I don't want to be alive? Where did I go wrong?

Amazingly, I wasn't injured from the incident and was not charged. The driver – who I'm pretty sure I walked past in the Gardaí station on the Tuesday afterwards – opted not to press charges but simply asked about my wellbeing. I could have ruined his life, yet he was willing to forgive and forget.

I had to do something similar. I had to accept responsibility for my actions. Before doing that, though, I went back to that bar a few days later in search of CCTV footage of the incident. I guess I was looking for confirmation that it really happened. As if that would change anything – the past or the present.

If I were to retrace my steps in search of the original trigger point in wanting to kill myself it would lead to a Venn diagram that interlinks all of my self-doubt, loss of confidence and burning anxiety back to when a childhood friend tragically lost her life in an accident.

The shock of experiencing something so traumatic at such a young age – I would have been around 15 at the time – is something that I never properly dealt with. I never really mourned her death or figured out how to put it to one side in my memory bank. Life isn't a movie that skips forward to a happy ending. The struggle is real and it is an everyday thing.

When you accept that you have mental health problems, you have to carefully tiptoe through life because any mis-step can result in a landmine going off. There are so many triggers surrounding you at all times that it's almost impossible not to explode every once in a while.

That is precisely what happened to me one week prior to my first suicide attempt. It was a close friend's going-away party as she prepared to move to Australia with her boyfriend, and everyone was in good spirits. Except I was nowhere to be found. The night before was a heavy one which ended in two guys carrying me back home because I was so out of it. They ended up in my kitchen chatting to my mum until all hours as I collapsed on the sofa having drunk way too much.

Naturally, I was in some state the next morning. Even though I was babysitting my niece, Emily, my mind was scattered, more focused on the fact that I could not find a single cent in my bag or any of my clothes. On top of that, my mobile phone was broken, again. I did somehow have a ticket to a rave concert that day, so it was a case of figuring out how to scramble together some funds to aid my next top-up on alcohol. As ever in these circumstances I would find a way to get what I wanted, whether it was through begging, stealing or borrowing. All that mattered to me was having a good time.

Once again I turned to Mum and mumbled a request, or was it a demand, to drop me to a bus stop.

Little did she know that I had snatched a bottle of wine from the fridge and transferred it to an empty water bottle. All that mattered was me having a good night out and I would use anyone and everyone to achieve that, even my poor old mum.

I can't remember what I consumed at the concert, drink or drugs or a combination of both, but it was probably enough to drop a horse. The next thing I know I'm turning up to my friend's party. The clock has struck past midnight and in I tumble with my rags for clothes and aroma of pure alcohol and the eyes hanging out of my head. Nobody was pleased to see me.

I had lied and lied, through my teeth, about where I was and why I had missed a special friend's party. As I stumbled through my local pub to make my way to the smoking area at the back, I could see faces with expressions of utter disgust stare in my direction and hear comments uttered in low tones but loud enough for their loaded adjectives to sting like whips to my back as I passed by. I ignored them, mainly because I knew that they were right, that I was a disgrace, but I didn't want to face up to reality at that moment.

However, the worst was still to come. After finally locating my friends – who felt in a way that their night was ruined by my selfish actions – they didn't hold back. Among the tirade volleyed in my direction was the cruellest but most realistic thing anyone had ever called me – a junkie. I couldn't believe that I had slipped so far down in their estimation that I was now being described as a junkie. That hurt more than anything I had gone through before. I had lost the respect of my friends and it was 100 per cent my fault.

That was the tipping point and it was a long time coming. I wasn't in control anymore, it was the drink and drugs that had taken over and I couldn't stop.

If those who I loved and cared for didn't want me around them then what was the point in trying anymore? I had already started to neglect the tasks assigned by my sponsor at the Drug and Alcohol Rehabilitation Centre, I wasn't playing football and any sort of future where I would be happy felt like an impossible dream.

My plan for committing suicide became active and when it comes to that stage there is no going back.

On the Monday after that party, I sat on a wall, sipping on a cup of coffee, smoking a cigarette and coming to agreement with the devil on my shoulder that my time on this Earth was done. I began to type into the Notes app on my phone what would be my goodbye message as tears streamed down my face.

2

Juggling It All

B EFORE the end – or attempted end –
there was a beginning. So let's rewind a
little.

In this social media-led world where everything
is filtered and edited to present the glossy versions of
our lives, I wanted to show the real me.

We've all been there: feeling down in the
dumps, slumped in an armchair and having our
misery compounded by envying the seemingly
picture perfect lives that others lead. Believe me,

that is the worst thing you can do when feeling down – start comparing yourself to others. What you really need is to see others, especially those who are successful in different areas, when they are at their most vulnerable. Not in a cruel kind of way, but more to realise that they too can have bad days.

The only issue is that nobody wants to reveal a side to themselves that isn't perfect. Imagine how powerful it would be to see your idol, or anyone you admire, reveal what they look like without makeup on or when they are hungover. Imagine how powerful it would be to see someone who you think has it all made for them in a miserable state that you can relate to. That is what I wanted to do with this book.

When going through my most difficult periods, I longed to have someone to look up to. I craved to find that someone who could show me that they had been through something similar to me and come out the other side. Young females are not going to expose themselves to that, and I understand why, but it's also the reason why I feel it's important that I share my experiences – in full – with the world.

It is really a shame that there are no books on the shelves of our local bookstore that cater for girls and young women looking for a role model to help them understand what it's like dealing with mental health issues. That is why this book exists, to be among the first to break that mould and scream out to young females that someone else has gone through the same things you are experiencing and there is a way of juggling it all to ultimately live a happier life.

Perhaps the first step in achieving that is finding balance. I've always been terrible at saying no to people. When I was in my early teens, I was playing three different sports and I felt like I was pulled and dragged left, right and centre. My wellbeing wasn't being looked after. As a person, nobody seemed to care. Everyone just wanted a piece of the sporting star. I allowed it to happen because I didn't want to let anyone down.

One of the things that I've learned is that it's OK to be selfish. In fact, you need to be selfish at times. That doesn't mean not sharing, or being cruel to others, it means looking after yourself. If you cannot look after your own health then there is no way that you can help others or be the best version of yourself. I've learned that the hard way.

Similar to a lot of kids, I played many different sports but I gravitated towards soccer, camogie and Gaelic football. It feels weird referring to football as soccer but anyone from Ireland will understand that sometimes you need to use it depending on your surroundings. Certainly growing up in County Cork, the influence of Gaelic games – including Gaelic football and camogie – is massive. Gaelic football is similar to soccer except you use your hands and can kick the ball between two posts, like a rugby goal, to earn a point or into the net, like a soccer goal, for three points. Camogie, however, is using a stick called a hurley and striking a ball called a sliotar. The same scoring system applies but it is a much quicker, more physical game. There is something almost barbaric yet poetic about camogie at the same time. I loved playing it.

It's probably difficult for people outside of Ireland to understand how important Gaelic games are. They bring local communities and towns together, they give you a sense of local pride, they teach you how to take a wallop and how to give one back, plus they provide an important link to Irish culture. If you are from a small town in Ireland, it's very likely that you grow up proud of where you come from and of your local GAA club.

I was lucky enough to be selected to play for Cork in both Gaelic football and camogie at a young age. It was a thrill to pull on that red jersey, to represent the Rebel County. Yet it was always at the expense of missing out on soccer or having to find a way to juggle it all.

I can't tell you how stressful it is to feel the pressure of friends when all you are trying to do is the right thing.

Around the same time that I was starting to break into the Cork set-up in camogie, my soccer – OK, I've had enough of this, it's football and that's what I'm sticking to from here on out. Anyway, my football career was also beginning to flourish. I had just come back from two tournaments with the Republic of Ireland under-17s and I was immediately promoted up to the under-19 squad with manager Dave Connell.

In my mind, I wanted to keep it all going; football, camogie, hanging out with my friends, going to school. Except it was all getting too much for me. And it came to a head, oddly enough, when Cork advanced to the All-Ireland Final and I had a decision to make.

There was an under-19 international camp scheduled for the same weekend and that meant I had to choose between playing for Cork at Croke Park or continuing my development as a footballer and staying in the mix with Ireland. I made a phone call to Dave Connell and said, 'Look, I know we've got a camp on this weekend but I also have an All-Ireland Final on the Sunday. Is it OK for me to go?'

There was a bit of friction on the back of that, not an argument but a bit of awkwardness because he saw it as representing your country and I completely understood that, but playing in the camogie final was something that I really wanted to do. We came to an agreement that I would train with the under-19s on the Friday and Saturday before being let go on the Sunday to meet up with the camogie team in the hotel.

We had fitness training on the Friday and I was knackered after that, and then there was a double session on the Saturday. It didn't feel like any ordinary training camp, it was more like a boot camp. I was glad to see my mum when she collected me from the Athletic Union League Complex that Saturday. We went straight to the hotel to meet up with the camogie team and I was exhausted. Not the best way to prepare for any game, never mind an All-Ireland Final.

The girls from the under-19 squad sent on their best wishes and I think the players and staff watched the game on TV. So it was great to know that they were cheering me on. And it was a fantastic experience to feature in the game – even though we lost to Wexford. Running out on to the Croke Park pitch was something else; it was such a big stadium. Not that I had much time to take it all in because the game was so fast and Wexford were so physical.

SCORING GOALS IN THE DARK

Within the first couple of minutes I got an almighty shoulder to my chest from my marker that sent me crashing down to the pitch, face first, trying to catch my breath. This was my introduction to an All-Ireland Final.

That was a great Cork team at the time, with legends such as Briege Corkery, Anna Geary, Rena Buckley and Gemma O'Connor, all of these amazing players who I had the privilege to play with. So as a 17-year-old I was always trying to fit in. Largely the girls were great to me but I know that some of the players in the squad were not too happy about someone 'floating in' from another sport. All I wanted to do was play.

Of course, after the final there was a massive drinking session and I followed the group, trying to keep up with them. It felt like there was no end to it, so many drinks coming one after another. This was one contest that I couldn't drop out of. I had to show the girls that I was one of them and able to keep up.

Next thing I knew, I woke up the following morning to discover that one of the girls was trying to shave my eyebrows off. I guess that made me part of the team!

There was such a good atmosphere in that squad and it was amazing to be able to play with players of that calibre, even though I still had an aspiration to play football in the senior Ireland team at the same time. Deep down, I knew that I wasn't capable of balancing the different sports.

There was definitely a lot of pressure on me being a young girl and playing different sports at such a high level. It was overwhelming at times. I remember leaving early from the Cork camogie homecoming back in the city because I was due to play a cup final for Douglas Hall at Turner's Cross the next day. I had to go home to get as much sleep as possible. Even though I scored two goals in that game against Wilton, I was so tired that I couldn't even run. I had no energy left in my body and I was taken off after 70 minutes.

So that was a hectic weekend, in an international training camp, playing camogie in the All-Ireland Final and then playing a cup final, which was huge for my club. I was being pulled and dragged all over the place. Of course I didn't have the bravery to say no as I felt that I would let people down.

Naturally, it got to a stage where I ended up hating it. There were people calling me to say, 'We're going to lose this game if you don't play.' I had friends on each of the teams and I didn't want them to hate me because I wasn't there. I guess I was a people-pleaser and didn't really think of the consequences. I wanted to play, especially in that camogie final, but it was so messed up that I wasn't able to make the right decision so I just took on everything at the same time.

Eventually I chose football because that gave me a chance to go higher, to test myself and to possibly earn a career from it. Camogie would always be there at that level and I hope to go back to it someday. But my separation from camogie wasn't nice as a lot of people were starting to say quite mean things behind my back and my mum heard a lot of it. They were accusing me of taking the place of other players on the team – at my local club and in the county team – and not being worthy of pulling on the Cork jersey. When I saw that it was hurting my mum, I knew that I had to just stick with the one sport.

Sometimes people ask me if a girl should only play one sport and suggest that my experience points in that direction. I don't think there is a simple answer to that. Girls, and boys, should play as many sports as they can when they are young because you learn different skills and make lots of friends.

The problems only started to boil up for me when I reached the very top level – an All-Ireland Final versus an international camp. Not every kid is going to have that dilemma to worry about, so I would suggest that they continue playing all sports as long as they remain fun.

I still have a hurley in my apartment in Glasgow and will sometimes bring it out for a puck around in the park. The Scottish locals must be baffled as to what sport I'm practising but it reminds me of home and I love it. While I fully appreciate the life that football has given me, I sometimes wonder what sort of camogie career I might have had if I had made a different decision.

3

Drinking

I WAS living two different lives. There was
the person my friends saw and there was the
person (player) the football world saw. And
there was a massive divide between the two.

This Dr Jekyll and Mr Hyde syndrome was
fairly obvious to spot. For example, when I went on
nights out, I would be anxious and thinking, 'Oh, I
hope this person doesn't see me like this,' because I
was bumping into people and I was in a serious state.
I would often wake up the day after with the fear of

embarrassment for what I had done or what I had said to people.

In a nutshell, the person who my friends got to see – largely in dimly lit nightclubs and pubs – was bubbly, willing to give anything a go, wild and a massive liability. I was able to hide the anxiety, the lack of self-confidence and the never-ending stream of doubt that I felt on most days. Pretend to be the happy-go-lucky person and throw down a few drinks so as not to remind myself that I was doing it.

The only problem was this persona could easily be seen in daylight and I was getting lazy switching back to someone who could act normally. This is when the drinking started to take over.

When I came back from Glasgow City – who I originally joined in 2015 – I signed with Cork City and one of my best friends, Amanda Budden, was called up to the Ireland national team squad in November 2017. I should have been involved in that squad too but I was nowhere fit enough and had been struggling with a few niggling injuries.

Instead I joined a few of my friends in making the trip to the Netherlands to support the girls. This turned out to be quite a significant game as Ireland held the reigning European champions to a 0-0 draw in front of a sold-out crowd. This was not what normally happened with Irish teams against the heavyweight nations, so it was a truly memorable night for all of the players and staff involved. For me, it is something that I can only remember in patches because I was so drunk during it.

I started drinking from early on that day. When we got to the stadium I had a bottle of wine in my bag and we were among the Irish supporters, who were mainly made up of parents of the players, who would have known me. I should have been on my best behaviour in front of them, yet there I was in the middle of them intoxicated, screaming and shouting words that didn't make sense but in my mind were words of encouragement to the players down on the pitch. I've no doubt that those parents were looking at me and thinking, 'What's after happening to her?'

The game itself was a blur. I know, mainly from highlights, that the girls produced a great performance but at the time I was simply riding a wave. That wave saw me drift down the steps of the stadium at full time to the advertising boards so that I could get closer to the players as they came across to celebrate with their families.

The first person to spot me was Katie McCabe. I was so proud of her and reached out to hug her. Katie took a step back and said, 'Jeez, you stink of drink.' I said something about being on my holidays as if to dismiss it and we moved on, celebrating with other players one by one. The weird thing about it was that I was celebrating from the other side of the barrier, not among the girls on the pitch.

Then I saw Colin Bell, the manager. I had been trying to avoid him so he didn't see me in the state that I was in. I thought that if he saw me drunk like that then I would never play international football again. It's a strange thing to have such conflicting emotions, of almost accepting that your slide down from the top was too much to ever come back from and yet also holding out a sliver of hope that it could still be achieved. Colin didn't come over, thankfully. He waved to me from a distance. But I'm sure that he noticed that I was two stone overweight, because I looked so bloated. My face was swollen from the amount of drink that I was consuming. I was an absolute mess.

Even the embarrassment of Katie, my long-time friend, essentially calling me out for being drunk did nothing to change my ways. Several months later I was back in the same situation. Amanda had been told that she would start in an international against

41

Northern Ireland; it would be her senior debut and I wasn't going to miss that.

So, again, I set off with a few friends for the game. This time it was in Dublin at Tallaght Stadium, but it might as well have been played on Pluto for all that I can remember of it. What I do recall is going straight to the Maldron Hotel across the road from the stadium before the match. I already had five or six pints onboard, then at half-time we went back across to the hotel to get more drink so I was fairly out of it during the second half.

At the end of the game we went down the steps towards the front to see Amanda and congratulate her. Ireland had won 4-0 and Amanda had kept a clean sheet, so I was delighted for her. But the first person I saw was Katie, so I reached out and gave her a big hug. Just like déjà vu, she said something about the smell of drink on me. It wasn't that she looked at me in disgust, but it was more like a realisation for her as to how bad things had become for me.

There was a period when Katie and I were inseparable. We played in the same Ireland underage teams, we played in the same team at Raheny United, we went to Glasgow City on trial together and we had a really good relationship. She was my best friend whenever I was involved with Ireland camps and we spoke every single day.

But when I saw her that day our relationship was not what it had been; I had started to lose connection with people because once I left Glasgow it was as if football didn't matter as much anymore. At the same time, Katie had signed for Arsenal; she was Ireland captain and her career was on the way up. I didn't want to bombard her with my problems at that time because she had so much on her plate, albeit different pressures to what I was experiencing.

When Katie took over as Ireland captain and I watched her lead the team out, I caught myself thinking, 'What am I doing with my life?' I could have, and should have, been on that team. But I wasn't looking after myself. It was something that I kind of accepted, as if a career in football was drifting away from me.

I looked at Katie with mixed emotions. On one hand I was delighted for her, on the other I wanted to be there alongside her. Katie, just like a lot of girls on the Ireland team, sacrificed so much to get to that stage in her career and I admire anyone who makes it to senior level because that really is the pinnacle in football, to represent your country.

So the least painful option was for me to drown out that disappointment of not being involved. Drinking was easier rather than facing the real reasons behind why I was falling behind.

Those two games, where I went to support my friends, turned out to be two standout moments. When I eventually went into treatment and started to look back on things that I regretted those were two days that definitely stood out. As part of my recovery, I had to accept that I couldn't change what had happened, all I could do was focus on putting it right in the future.

So when I went back to Glasgow and started playing well again, I got back into the Ireland set-up and that really caught me by surprise because I thought that that would never happen. Part of that process was me looking at myself and asking how I allowed the drink to take over my life.

I really am a completely different person when I'm drinking. I lower my standards so much. It happens to everyone, but it's something that completely takes over me. When drinking, I have no self-awareness and no respect for anyone. In fact, I have no respect for myself when drinking; if I did then I wouldn't have turned up to those two international games. I knew that current and former managers were going to be there, parents of other players, FAI staff members who had helped me through the years and the players too, who I would consider to be friends. Even the fans, who would previously have looked up to me and supported me. A while after that second game, someone tagged me in a photo on Twitter. It was of two people in Tallaght Stadium but I didn't recognise who the girl was. It was me. Or at least an intoxicated version of me.

I suppose that period showed how much my life had changed. The fact that I didn't even recognise myself in a photo was surely a sign that things had gone too far. It was always about me crying out for help but, at the same time, being afraid to ask for it. That's why when I drank it would mostly be in a social setting, as if I wanted to be around people and for them to want to be around me.

I was never comfortable with myself. I was never in shape. I was never comfortable in my body, ever. I don't know if that comes from my sexuality or things like that. Growing up, I was always playing with the boys and I kind of rejected being with the girls. The reason for that was because I felt like an outcast among the girls, that they were just so different to me. They would go out and look nice with their makeup on, but I was the complete opposite. That was something that I always struggled with when growing up. It is why drinking helped, to an extent, to take me out of that mindset. Although the real world was waiting for me every time.

Then again, the real world did remind me, at times, that I could thrive in it. A good example would be when I've met up with the Ireland senior squad through the years. When the squad assembles on the first day, you have players coming from different parts of the world and it is almost like a family being reunited. Maybe it is our Irishness or just the bonds that we strike, but there is always a great feeling when we get together.

So missing out on international squads has really hurt me, from a footballing perspective of not playing and proving myself at a higher level, but also from a social aspect of missing out on that connection with girls who I've literally grown up with.

When I got my first senior cap, in 2015 against Spain, I said to myself, 'Wow, this is amazing. I never want to lose this feeling.' The only time that I matched that feeling was when I was drinking. So I was always looking for that high. Even that extraordinary high against Spain was quickly followed by a slump as I went out drinking with some of the players after the game and was in such a horrible state that I missed my flight back to Glasgow the next day. Here I was making my senior debut for my country and instantly undoing the work that had gotten me there in the first place. I could never find the balance between the two. I'm an all-or-nothing kind of person.

It all came to a point where I felt it was life or death. Either I fix this or it's over. Quite simply, I had to find that balance.

It would take some time, though, for me to build up the courage to tackle my demons. I had to concede, to tap out, to admit that I needed help before a change could come. I had to admit that drinking was killing me.

No matter how many times family and friends tell you the right thing, you still need something else to motivate you towards truly making a change. I suppose my Ireland career was that catalyst in a way. Since I was a kid I had always wanted to wear that green jersey and be the best that I could be. And, if I'm being honest, it all came too easily for me. From what I experienced at underage level and then making my senior debut, I had achieved a hell of a lot in a short period of time.

Life goes on with or without football. At the end of my career, I'd love to be able to look back and be able to say that I reached my potential. But when you're sitting in your local pub watching your friends play for their clubs on TV then it puts everything into context. If you choose the drink then prepare to suffer the consequences.

Drinking came too easily to me. I shouldn't really have had any place in a local pub in the middle of the day where the usual crew consisted of retired men but I didn't care. I enjoyed a pint of beer as much as an older man might and that was completely wrong. I'm not sure how I even developed a taste for it, but drinking became part of my life as much as playing football or eating my dinner was. In the back of my mind I knew that it wasn't right but I didn't want to give up my place on that bar stool.

Walk inside most pubs and you will be struck by how dark it is. Some enter in a bid to hide themselves away from the world, others to connect with friends. I suppose I wanted a little of both. The real world was left outside the door once you stepped up to that bar and ordered your first drink. At that point you are joining an exclusive club, which has one rule: you can only join the conversation if you have a drink in your hand. It didn't matter about my age or gender, I was one of those and I could drink with the best of them.

I knew that I was good at playing football and I discovered that I was also good at drinking alcohol. Well, except for when I took it too far by having one too many. And that was quite often.

4

Rising Star

PLAYING above my age grade was something that I had always done. Whether it was on the local green near my house with the boys or with my local club, Douglas Hall, I would regularly be one of the youngest involved.

Nowadays, parents will want to protect their kids by having them only playing for a girls team at the appropriate age level, and that's fine. But I know that playing with boys and against older girls definitely helped my development as a player. In fact, it fast-tracked me.

Without being coached on it, I learned how to receive the ball into feet when someone was marking me closely, how to spin away from them, how to pick myself back up if fouled and how to act around older kids. While I was just having fun playing, those days playing with the boys proved to be invaluable as my footballing career quickly took off.

If I'm being honest, that is the environment I felt most comfortable in. Playing with dolls and dressing up nice just didn't interest me. Give me a summer's day going on some sort of adventure that ended up with my arms cut from thorn bushes, my knees scraped from falling off my skateboard and my runners caked in mud. One of my favourite things growing up was a game called manhunt, which was a more aggressive version of hide and seek. I loved being out there among the boys and when they played football that felt like a natural thing to do as well.

I still had my female friends and as I got older I played other sports, particularly Gaelic football and camogie. Oh, and how could I forget winning the Community Games with Douglas GAA? I was the only girl on the team and I remember one of the boys trying to pull my hair to stop me. I guess he didn't want me showing him up. But once you get your acceptance on the pitch, everything is much easier off it because I wasn't treated differently for being a girl playing with boys; rather I was embraced for it.

In my estate, Broadale, kids were everywhere, always out playing. Whether they were on a bicycle, rollerblades or playing games like tip the can, it felt like kids were out each summer day from morning to night having fun. Of course there was always a game of football to be had too.

We created a mini World Cup tournament between the different roads in our estate. There was the Circle, the Downs, the Drive and the Crescent. I was from the Circle and we would always win, mainly because I had my next-door neighbour Mark on my team, as well as Ian and Stephen.

Sometimes I would try to spice things up by asking Big Dave Barry – a Cork City legend who famously scored against Bayern Munich – to join us. Those were great days, endless days of fun. The only time we stopped playing, it seemed, was when the ice cream van came around or when we dashed across to the Broadale Stores to exchange our 5p and 10p coins for a bag full of the best jellies in Cork.

We tried to upgrade things one day by asking my dad, who worked on a construction site, and Mark's dad Aidan – who is effectively my second dad – to build us a stadium. It didn't happen but that did not stop us from imagining scoring our goals in our own our Theatre of Dreams.

From countless hours playing on the local green, I built up long-lasting friendships with Shane, Gavin and Liam. They were from different roads so sometimes they were the enemy on the pitch, but we were always able to have a laugh afterwards. The laughing has never stopped among us, especially since our tradition of meeting up every Christmas Day brings those fond memories rushing back.

Where I grew up in the Circle, the families – the Clarkes, the Crowleys, the O'Regans and the O'Connors – all looked after each other. Even going home now, it's as if nothing has changed because that sense of community has stood the test of time. Sport was something that brought us all together and if we ever get to have a big reunion I bet there will be plenty of stories of our childhood told that will embarrass my friends and me.

Graduating from our local green to club level with Douglas Hall went smoothly with the help of Dave Barry. I always had lots of male friends around me who believed I could go all the way. I know he would probably agree but my next-door neighbour Mark taught me everything that I know.

My first football tournament was with Douglas Hall under-nines, where I scored over 20 goals, won the golden boot as the top goalscorer and was named player of the tournament. It attracted the attention of the Lakewood AFC chairman, who was trying to recruit me, but Noreen Martin stepped in to wave him away. Noreen was in charge of the girls' section at Douglas Hall and was effectively my football mammy – always there for me.

I think the team environment suited me. It's a place where individuals can stand out or hide behind someone else if a bit shy – that worked for me because I wanted both of those at different times.

I guess that my club career went better than expected because it wasn't long before I was getting called up for international football.

I was only 13 years old when I first represented the Republic of Ireland at under-15 level and then I was 15 when called into the under-17s. At the time I didn't take much notice of my rise but looking back now I can appreciate how much faith coaches showed in me. Noel King and Harry Kenny were running the under-17s at that time; they had so many good players to call on but they showed a lot of trust in me at such a young age and I'm grateful for that opportunity.

One of the perks that comes with playing international football is that you get to travel to places you never thought you would visit. With the under-17s, I was the baby of the group so I didn't expect much game time. The team had got through the first phase of qualifying and I was then selected for the second phase, which meant travelling out to Ukraine.

I was just happy to be involved. That isn't selling myself short or anything, I knew that I was the rookie player being brought along to soak up the experience of it all and that was fine with me.

We had a few Cork girls involved in the squad, which definitely helped me, in Amanda Budden, Denise O'Sullivan and Rebecca Kearney. They played their club football with Wilton United and Lakewood Athletic but we all got on and Amanda and I grew to be best friends. That is a huge part of international football too, making friends for life.

You spend so much time together travelling on buses and planes, staying in hotels for weeks on end, training sessions, matches, eating together at every meal; you are always with the same people so it's vital that you get along.

In Ukraine, we had to get an armed escort to the airport such was the dangerous environment we were in at the time. It's funny what memories stick with you because the main thing that comes to mind about our three games in Ukraine is that we were stranded afterwards due to the volcanic ash cloud that came from Iceland in 2010 and grounded all flights.

Again, we topped our group with wins over Ukraine and Sweden, plus a draw with Poland. That was an exceptionally talented squad with the likes of Grace Moloney, Megan Campbell, Ciara Grant, Dora Gorman, Denise O'Sullivan, Siobhan Killeen, Rianna Jarrett and Aileen Gilroy. Both Ciara and Dora would go on to become fully qualified doctors. I'm not sure what the average number of players are who go on to win senior caps from any underage squad, but this one was quite exceptional in that regard. At last count, 12 of the girls made it all the way to senior level while many others should have too but life can take you in unexpected directions at times – as I know all too well!

Just two months after those games in Ukraine, we were going to the UEFA European Championship in Nyon, Switzerland. I had just turned 15 so the official notification of my call-up arrived via an email to my mum. That gave me something to boast about in school.

If I'm being honest, I just went with the flow of it all. I don't think I understood what a European Championship was at that time. It probably only sunk in that this was a big deal when the media attention came before the final, with the girls getting interviewed, family telling us about pieces in the newspapers back home and stuff about us on RTÉ television.

At that point, I started to pay more attention. Little things stood out, like the footballs were all branded with the tournament logo and having my name on the back on my jersey for the first time. It was so professional. A few of the girls on our team were studying for their Leaving Certificate, while I had just done my Junior Certificate. It was mad that we were all part of the one squad.

Having topped our group in Ukraine, we were one of four teams left so it was a straight knockout tournament in Nyon. We were there for two weeks overall and had Germany in our semi-final. It was a tense game with Megan Campbell getting the only goal – a long-range free kick – and that was unreal. We held on to set up a final with Spain.

It's probably important to emphasise how big of an achievement this was. Little old Ireland didn't qualify for major tournaments, let alone reach semi-finals and finals. This was brand-new ground that we were treading and the world was starting to take notice. Forget about the Fighting Irish, we were now showing that we were the Skilful Irish and we could give anyone a game. We were fearless as all we knew was winning, so the history of Irish teams who had gone before us and fallen down for various reasons did not even enter our thoughts.

My uncle lived in Geneva at the time so my family went over and stayed with him. That was great to have them over there supporting me, even if I was on the bench and unlikely to feature. This was a big deal for everyone involved and I felt that even more once we qualified for the final. Suddenly the hype cranked up and everyone was buzzing.

The final itself was another tight game. Spain had a lot of quality players, including Alexia Putellas, who would go on to win the Women's Ballon d'Or in 2021. We had some excellent players too and we pushed them all the way to a penalty shoot-out but we came up just short. It was disappointing to lose but we all knew just how well we had done.

We didn't know it then but it was the first time that an Ireland women's team had qualified for a major tournament, let alone finish as runners-up. And it's the only medal that I've picked up for playing for my country to date. I still have that silver medal and my jersey!

As a result of being involved in that European Championship, we qualified directly for the FIFA Women's Under-17 World Cup which was held in September that year in Trinidad and Tobago. That experience was unreal. The hotel we were staying in, the rooms that we had, the size of beds and it was my first time ever getting paid. We got an envelope and I think there was €200 in it, but I can't remember what I spent it on.

I got to feature in the tournament too when I got on for about 15 minutes as a substitute in the first group game against Brazil. We lost that 2-1 then we beat Canada and Ghana to reach the quarter-finals. For the match against Ghana, we had to fly from Trinidad to Tobago and it was in one of those small propeller planes. For someone who isn't fond of flying that was not something I want to go through again.

In Tobago we stayed in shacks, the doors didn't even close, and then every hour on the hour the Ghana team would come out and start praying together. I was thinking, 'How are they going to play a game after being up all night praying?' But that was a great exposure to different cultures and it really opened up my eyes to how people from other countries acted. We were all girls around the same age but shaped by our different backgrounds.

There was a great atmosphere around our squad. Noel and Harry were great at lifting the mood and the whole experience really gave me a feel for what it is like to play for your national team. We lost 2-1 to Japan in the quarter-final but, just like losing to Spain in the Euro final, there was no shame in it. We gave it everything and we enjoyed it.

It would be another four years before I made it back to a major tournament, this time with the under-19s in Norway with Dave Connell and Dave Bell. It's not that I was taking it for granted, but I probably didn't appreciate then how much of an achievement it was to be part of those squads. And then to get the results that we did – we beat Spain, England and Sweden in our group to reach the semi-finals. To do that was just unreal. All higher-ranked teams, yet we beat them and deserved to beat them.

I think a lot of that came down to the fact that we were such a close-knit team. Again, just like our under-17 squad from a few years before, there were ten players, including myself, who would go on to win senior caps. The likes of Katie McCabe, Sarah Rowe and Amy O'Connor have become genuine superstars, even though Sarah and Amy are doing it in Aussie rules and Gaelic football, and camogie, respectively. It was about more than our individual talent though. There is a humility to Irish teams that can be a real asset when combined with desire and talent. I think we had all of those things and it's why we beat those teams.

For me, that tournament is one that I will always treasure. I had broken my leg in April, playing for Raheny United, and it looked as though my chances of making the Ireland squad were over. But I was determined to be involved and our manager, Dave Connell, took a chance on me. We knew the potential consequences of a reoccurrence, but nothing was going to stop me from playing in those games just two months after the original injury.

Then I scored in our opening game against Spain and I cannot really do justice in describing the swell of emotions that ran through me. I remember striking the ball, seeing it hit the back of the net and

67

running away to celebrate, all the while thinking, 'I've just scored against Spain.' That goal felt like justification for the hard work I put in, for believing in myself and for Dave in trusting me. I still get goosebumps when I think back to it.

That was the first time that I realised the power of social media. All of the messages that came through, the coverage of our game, the different people reacting to what we had done, it was crazy to see it all.

When I look back at that tournament, I have nothing but good memories. One of my favourites was when all of the players came together around a piano in the hotel lobby to sing at the top of our lungs. Earlier in the day, there was a bit of drama as some of the players wanted to use our day off to visit a local shopping centre while others wanted to go into the city centre. Dave Connell didn't react well to that at all. He said that if we did anything it should be together, that if we were not together in everything that we did then we wouldn't be a team on the pitch and be able to rely on each other. He was 100 per cent right but at the time we just wanted to be teenage girls.

So the coaching staff went out for a coffee and left us players in the hotel to figure it out ourselves. We all drifted across the road from our hotel to a lake, where *Sportsfile* photographer Stephen McCarthy took some photos and we started to have a bit of a laugh. Then we got back to the hotel and Ciara O'Connell sat down at the piano, in the main lobby. She was excellent on piano and guitar, so she started to play 'Read All About It' by Emeli Sandé and each of the girls gathered around to sing along. It was a really special moment where we showed that we truly were a team.

What made it even more significant was that the coaching staff arrived back in the middle of it.

They couldn't believe what they were seeing. When they left the hotel earlier that day they were worried about possible fractions in the squad, but then they came back and see us all singing together. A few tears were shed. It was just this lovely moment that happened by chance.

Funnily enough, the way that the hotel was built meant that noise from the lobby went straight up and people on every level could hear it. So we looked up during our singing and could see the other teams peering over the balcony of each floor, watching us. I think they thought we were half mad, singing as a group in the middle of the afternoon. But they all clapped once we finished, the Spanish, the Dutch and the Norwegians.

The Irish teams never need much encouragement for a sing-song. And in fairness to managers like Dave Connell and Noel King they created really welcoming environments for us to feel comfortable in. There is a lot of tension involved in international football and you can lose a game before it even kicks off if you don't have the balance right off the pitch. Thankfully, more often than not we did.

Around that time, a lot of people were referring to me as a 'rising star' and it was nice to hear that. Football, though, can be cruel as it's all about what have you done lately. You scored a goal in the European Championship, but what's next? And the pressure that came with that was something I wasn't ready for because I wasn't looking after myself properly.

Your status as a 'rising star' can only last so long. There will always be others itching to take your place. So while I started the tournament with that goal against Spain, it was another player who had everyone talking when we played against the Netherlands in the semi-finals. And after scoring a hat-trick in a 4-0 win over us, that was the beginning of Vivianne Miedema becoming one of the stars of women's football. She was at Bayern Munich then but would go on to become one of the world's best players at Arsenal – ironically enough with Katie McCabe setting up many of her goals – and with the Dutch team.

The semi-final proved to be too much for us. A few players had niggling injuries, we were all physically exhausted having just beaten Sweden three days before and Miedema was in unstoppable form. That golden summer in Norway, where we were nicknamed 'The History Girls', ended with a crushing defeat but we were all proud of reaching the semi-finals and there was a big welcoming party at Dublin Airport for when we eventually got home.

Even though we didn't go all the way or reach the final, it was still a fitting end to my underage career. Next up was senior football for club and country.

5

From High to Low
to Going Pro

WHEN you are on a high, everyone wants a piece of you. Or at least that's how it feels.

It was only two weeks after the UEFA Women's Under-19 European Championship that I was back in action at an elite level with UEFA Women's Champions League qualifiers.

From the thrill of reaching the Euro semi-finals to being involved in the top club competition in women's football, this was the stuff of dreams. I had just turned 19 years old yet these career highs were coming at me as if it was something that happened every week.

The only problem was that I didn't want to know about it. When I got the call that Raheny United would travel out to Romania for three Champions League qualifiers, I felt sick in my stomach and wanted to hide under my bed covers. Maybe it was fatigue, or not having fully recovered from the leg break just five months previous. Or maybe it was the comedown from the Euros and the session that we had afterwards.

Having returned home from the Euros, all of the players were on a high. There must have been 100 people at the airport to greet us, the RTÉ cameras were there, photographers were snapping away; it was like we had won the tournament. So the players decided to keep the party going. A few of us rented an apartment in Dublin city centre and the drinking started very early.

I think we got into the apartment for two o'clock and by the time it was four o'clock I could barely see, I was that drunk. I was fighting with everyone and then I passed out on the bed. So I didn't even make it out into town. Instead, I slept through most of the night before eventually falling out of the bed and slicing the back of my ear when one of my earrings got tangled up. There was blood everywhere and two of the younger players, Amanda McQuillan and Keeva Keenan, helped me. I still have a small scar behind my ear to remind me of that night.

So it's safe to say that I was in no fit state to go into three key Champions League games. I probably should have taken a couple of weeks to rest and recover.

Typical of what I have always done, however, I just got on with it. Not wanting to let people down, I packed my bags and travelled with the Raheny squad to the far side of Europe. My mum, I'm sure, would have been glad to get rid of me as I did nothing but moan for two weeks about not wanting to go and then I ended up going.

Quite often football has been the remedy, or at least the short-term distraction, that I need to keep my mental health under control. So it was probably a good thing for me to be involved in those games.

Not that I showed much enthusiasm. My room-mate, Noelle Murray, gave me a new nickname of 'Sleeping Bag' because I was always asleep. If we weren't travelling somewhere or eating or training or playing a match then I would be in bed. Pull the curtains, curl up under the covers and allow a deep sleep to push the negative thoughts away. Except that is no way for a senior footballer to act, and that is exactly what I was.

I still took part in training and played in the games, but I really didn't want to be there. It's hard to describe loving something, as I do with football, yet not wanting to be around it at a time when one of the best opportunities for any player had come around. Of course, I didn't dare tell anyone how I felt. I couldn't make sense of it. So I just got on with it.

In our first game against Olimpia Cluj, who were the hosts, I scored with about ten minutes to go with the match locked at 1-1. So that winner gave us three points and set us up nicely for the next game against Bulgarian side NSA Sofia two days later. Everything was just falling to me as I scored twice to record a 2-0 win and bring it all into our last group game. We had one extra day of rest before taking on Maltese side Hibernians, who shocked us by taking an early lead but Catherine Cronin pulled one back and then I scored another late goal. Three games, four goals, nine points and qualification to the knockout phase. Job done!

I loved the celebrations that followed because they allowed me to drown out how I was feeling. I had a great relationship with the girls at Raheny but something wasn't right – and that something was me.

The FAI and the state training board FÁS ran a football and education course – split into various centres around the country – with the intention of giving young footballers a chance to continue their development alongside earning a diploma to help them advance their careers or give them something to fall back on. It was something that proved quite popular, with the likes of Roy Keane doing the course before he left for Nottingham Forest as a teenager. By the time I had finished school, they were catering for female players too.

I had been on the course in Cork, which was run by Niall O'Regan, but it became a regular thing for me to call in sick every Monday having been out drinking all night on the Sunday following our games with Raheny. Forget about responsibility and long-term planning, even the mention of taking anything serious gave me a headache.

I needed help, that much was obvious. Eventually I decided to admit that to others so I spoke with the Raheny manager, Casey McQuillan, and told him that it was all getting to be too much for me. He listened to what I had to say and shared some advice but ultimately encouraged me to speak with someone professionally.

A lot of things started to slip away from me at that stage. I dropped out of a college course at the Carlow Institute of Technology as I was more interested in the party life than the education. I started to miss a lot of days and then began to have a recurring thought that I would be better off without football. Forget about being the 'rising star', I was burnt out.

After the Champions League games, I went into a bad tackle and ended up hurting my leg again. But I used that as an excuse as to how I was feeling. At that stage, I just didn't want to play football. It made me feel guilty because I was living in Raheny team-mate Siobhan Killeen's house in Dublin and her family helped me so much when I was playing for the club. I didn't want to let them down but there came a time when I just couldn't keep going.

Raheny had got through to the knockout phase in the Champions League, where they were pitted against Bristol Academy. A lot of people felt that we had a real chance against them because they weren't exactly one of the major teams in England. We were at home for the first leg, playing in Richmond Park for the first time, and everyone was excited. This was three years on from Peamount United facing Paris Saint-Germain at the same stage of the competition, so we wanted to go one better than they did.

Well, we got battered. From the opening ten minutes you could see the difference between a full-time and a part-time team. It was like they were operating at a different speed. Wales international Natasha Harding was outstanding, scoring twice, as Bristol won 4-0 but it would have been a lot worse if our goalkeeper, Niamh Reid-Burke, hadn't produced the game of her life.

I came on as a substitute on 55 minutes but I might as well not have bothered. I wasn't fit enough, I couldn't get into the rhythm of the game and I was just chasing shadows. Not much changed for the second leg except that they didn't punish us as badly. I didn't play in that one as Raheny lost 2-1 and the Champions League run came to an end.

I was still officially a student at Carlow, studying on Sports Management, but I never really gave it a fair shot. I wasn't in the right mind. I struggled the entire time and the drinking got worse when I stayed down there. There were a couple of occasions when I didn't go to the training sessions in the morning because I was too drunk from the night before. That was giving me a bad reputation and I didn't know how to stop it.

What was it with me? I didn't want to be in school because all I wanted to do was to play football. I didn't want to play football because all I wanted was a social life. I didn't want the social life when it became too much. And every time I tried to get involved with a job or education I couldn't last at it. Nothing seemed to work for me.

These weren't teenage tantrums though. I remember when I was at Carlow and feeling really suicidal. It was one of the first times that those thoughts were really severe. That was when I spoke with Casey and he came down to Carlow so we could talk with Paul O'Reilly and Luke Hardy, who ran the college course. It was time to go home.

When I returned home, I started seeing a doctor once a week. It should have been something that helped me get better but I didn't take it seriously. Some days I was still stinking of drink and not paying much attention, with Mum crying beside me. Mum didn't know what to do with me. Those were extremely dark times, especially for my family because they didn't know what was going to happen.

One day, Mum admitted that she held fears of the Gardaí arriving at the house someday to inform her that I was dead. I was actually sober when she said that, so it hit me hard. We were, probably for the first time, having an open conversation about everything. So I fully understood her feeling that way because it was always her who would be texting or calling me to see if I was OK, who picked me up from parties or friends' houses and who drove me to football or to the hospital. I guess she hoped that football could somehow get me on the straight and narrow towards some form of stability.

People have always seemed to have high expectations of me. I had achieved a lot up to a point but then it was almost as if I had forgotten about who I was and what I had done. It felt like everyone had a specific idea of my persona, but I felt completely different to whatever they came up with. I was doing well on the pitch, but off the pitch if anyone knew what I had been up to they would have had a very different opinion of me.

I struggled through the remainder of the season with Raheny but my leg injury got worse so I had to wear a protective boot, which ruled me out of the FAI Women's Cup Final in the Aviva Stadium. I was there on the pitch with the girls when they won, beating UCD Waves after extra time, and I went out with them afterwards to drink the night away. At the time it didn't register with me, but I was clearly more interested in the drinking session than the football match. And things were about to get a whole lot worse.

Just over a month later, on Christmas Eve, I hit rock bottom. Out of nowhere, or so it seemed at the time, I had a panic attack. My mum was all flustered and called the neighbours in to our house as they waited for the ambulance to come. They thought that I had overdosed on my medication. I had fallen out of my bed, I was rolling around on the ground, I couldn't breathe properly. This was the first time that I had had such a visible panic attack in front of anyone.

When the ambulance drivers arrived, they tried to steady me and were asking all sorts of questions. One of them was incredibly rude. He clearly thought that I was faking it because there were no signs of any drugs being taken. He was lecturing me about how I was hurting my family when all I could think of was, 'Why aren't you trying to help me?' That was a really horrible experience, to feel absolutely helpless and not know why at the same time when someone chooses to berate you for your behaviour.

The root of the problem? My mental health. It has always been my mental health. You never think it's going to be you, that you would be the one with the problem. You put up this false front as if such an illness could ever affect you. Except it does. It seeps into your pores, takes control of your inner voice and controls your decision-making. Mental health is no joke and I started to find that out the hard way.

As much I have blamed the drink through the years, it always leads back to my failure of dealing with my own mental health issues. I only got to realise that when I fully became sober. Up until then it was easy to blame the drink and that was the first step in tackling it – cutting out the drink.

I decided to finally get some help. My brother, Philip, was brilliant with this as he understood what I was going through and vowed to help me. He contacted Pieta, which is a fantastic place that helps people with all sort of mental health problems, and the process started. Admitting that I had a problem was the first part and that wasn't as easy to do as I thought it would be. Sure, I said the words when a counsellor asked, but I wasn't truly buying into it.

I'd say for the first six months of regular visits, I was in denial that I had a problem with drink. I always maintained that I could stop whenever I wanted to, it was just that I didn't really want to stop. Drinking was a hobby, it was a way of interacting with friends and it was something that almost motivated me to get out of the house and do something, as weird as that may sound.

If I wasn't stupid enough to be consuming the amount of alcohol that I was in my teenage years, I was also smoking cigarettes and by the time I was 20 drugs were involved. The drugs were never something that I was too worried about because I wasn't taking them with any kind of regularity, although they almost became the one thing that had the potential to ruin my life and any future plans of becoming a professional footballer.

Taking drugs to get high was one thing; taking them to zone out was another. I developed a dependency on smoking cannabis just to get to sleep on an average night because I was pumping so much into my system that I was hardwired for the majority of the day. It became a routine, where I had to wind down each night by smoking some weed, leaving for a couple of hours – usually to find food to snack on – and then coming back to zone out.

Of course, I didn't think anything of it. What harm was smoking a joint every so often? Little did I know that five years later my carefree attitude towards drugs would give me one of the biggest frights of my life.

On one weekend, I went to a music festival in Westmeath with some friends. I knew before leaving home that this was going to be one of my 'couldn't give a shit what happens' experiences. Naturally, there was plenty of drinking on the journey and by the time we arrived at the venue it already felt like something big was going to happen. There was a tension in the air with thousands of people in the same carefree mindset; this was a gathering of people to let go, lose themselves for the day and do whatever they wanted to do. With that in mind, I came armed with a pocket-full of drugs.

Standing in that muddy field, shuttling along in a never-ending queue, I could see that security men were doing searches on people. It didn't matter to me, though because I always found a way through tricky situations. There was almost a bravado element to my mindset of 'bring it on'. I was determined to have a good time and nobody was going to stop me.

Except that's not how things work in the real world. When you continually push things to the limit, there comes a time when you get smacked in the face with a reminder that there are rules. That is exactly what happened when an undercover Garda suddenly sprung up beside me, went through a very quick search and found my stash. Completely embarrassed, I was handed over to a police officer who ensured my anxiety rose another few levels by confirming that a letter would be sent to my home within six weeks.

I thought that would be it; if I officially got a criminal record then my future was over.

The weight of the negative thoughts I felt during that period was unbearable. Imagine waking up in the morning and not even having the motivation to put your socks on. What's the point in facing the world? I have nothing to give to it and it has nothing it wants to give to me. Those are the type of thoughts that swirl around inside your head when that devil appears on your shoulder to remind you of your worthlessness. Once the negativity gets a hold on you, it strangles every part of you. Your chest feels tight, your legs feel heavy, your eyes hardly open and your appetite disappears. Your contribution to life feels pointless.

The caution for the possession of drugs gave me a really bad fright about what way my life was going. There were many elements that were part of it, but a huge one was that question of, 'What am I doing with my life?' If this comes back to bite me in my ass it means I can't leave the country, everyone is going to know about it and my parents will kill me. That was all going through my head.

Then I decided that enough was enough. Ultimately you shape your own destiny and it takes a hell of a lot of honesty to admit that you are the maker of your own problems. So I sought out help, possibly for the first time that I truly wanted it, and I checked into the drug and alcohol centre, where I met Andrew who would become my sponsor and mentor. This was only the beginning, like laying out all of the pieces of a jigsaw on the floor and taking them piece by piece to figure out what approach will work best.

A daily routine was what I needed most. I needed to have a purpose to get out of bed each day. That started with eating better then going to the gym to work out and having some responsibilities to keep my mind active. Football wasn't really a priority at this stage, I just wanted to get my head clear and start on that road to recovery.

Typical of my luck, however, everything looked to be about to come crashing down in December, just when I had hit on a good rhythm with everything. I arrived home from the gym one day and the Gardaí were there with my court summons.

If I wasn't doing so well at that period it would have caused war inside my house but I wasn't drinking, I was back in the gym and I was taking it step by step. So Mum was very open with me about it because she didn't want that to be a trigger that led to me falling off the wagon again.

I got through that Christmas with the summons in the back of my mind. I didn't drink, I kept the fitness up and I was feeling good. Then I received a call about signing with Glasgow City. Except I couldn't do anything until I knew what was happening with the courts, because I didn't want to commit to signing with Glasgow then all of a sudden have to serve community service or be unable to leave the country. So I kept playing it off, saying that I was too busy with work – I had been doing some work with BodyFuelz, a health food company.

To be wanted by a club such as Glasgow City was huge. They were the best team in the Scottish Women's Premiership and were setting the benchmark for how a small club should be run on and off the pitch. They were producing players of immense talent who were being called into the Scotland national team and they were winning trophies every year.

If you could have measured my anxiety at that time it would have smashed the thermometer like how you see it in the cartoons. With my life seemingly back on track and a real option to turn professional, I had this stupid thing hanging over me.

And, as with everything, it was completely my fault. I had made up some stupid story to my parents about the drugs but they were mine. What was I doing with drugs? Such a stupid thing to do. The one thing that could end all of my hopes. All of these thoughts were racing through my head as my brother brought me up to the court in Westmeath.

There were about 15 or 20 people there for the same reason. The judge called us up one by one, you confirmed your name and then a verdict was given. Then it was my turn. My palms were sweaty, I was trying not to look at the floor all of the time, my chest felt tight and my breathing was all over the place. Thankfully, though, the judge was in a lenient mood when he said that the offence wasn't going on my record and that if I ever wanted to go abroad that it wouldn't be a problem. I got away with a €350 fine. The sense of relief was like nothing I had ever felt before, mainly because I was in such a good place at that time and doing so well. Finally, my life could get started.

I decided to sign for Glasgow. Except it wasn't that easy. I had been in recovery over the previous months and Andrew didn't think I was ready to make the move. So we agreed that I would fly over on a Friday for a game on Saturday and come home for the usual treatment. That was fine, except that I had to hide from the club that the real reason for me constantly going home was because I was in treatment to recover from alcohol addiction, not because I was homesick. That happened for about four weeks before we felt that I was finally ready to move full-time over to Glasgow.

What a rollercoaster year that was, full of highs and lows. But the adventure was only really beginning as I continued my journey into professional football.

All so innocent: With my older sister Ellen when butter wouldn't melt in my mouth

Always on the move: Getting ready to explore on my bike with Mark, my next door neighbour

Can't catch me: Playing against the boys in the GAA Community Games. I was so quick that one boy pulled me back by the hair!

Cork Abú: A proud day representing my county in the All-Ireland Camogie Final at Croke Park

Making the call: Sharing my exam results with my Mum whilst away in Trinidad at the FIFA Women's Under-17 World Cup

World Cup Fever: Getting to play at the FIFA WU17 World Cup against Brazil. What an incredible experience!

Get In There: Celebrating my goal against Spain in our opening game of the UEFA Women's Under-19 European Championships

All dressed up: Honoured to receive the FAI Women's Under-19 Player of the Year Award from Ireland striker Shane Long

Breakaway: In action for Raheny United against Jess Gargan of Peamount United in the Women's National League

Proud: My senior Republic of Ireland Women's National Team debut against Spain in Tallaght Stadium. A day that I won't ever forget

On Target: Getting the better of UCD Waves goalkeeper Brooke Dunne to score the winning goal for Cork City in the 2015 FAI Women's Cup Final at Aviva Stadium

Cue the Celebrations: What a feeling to win the FAI Women's Cup with my hometown club and a lot of life-long friends

Centre of Attention: Relieved and delighted in equal measure after scoring the winner in the Scottish Women's Cup Final in 2019

6

Glory, Glory Glasgow City

I'VE never left my comfort zone. There, I said it. And it's true. If I were to start my professional career in any place that most closely resembled home it would be Glasgow.

The weather is similar to Cork. The Scottish people are very welcoming, like the Irish. The sense of humour is what I'm used to.

The infrastructure and working-class lifestyle are the same. And it's only a short flight from one to the other.

When I first went over on trial with Katie McCabe, I was surprised that it wasn't all that different to what I had known up to that point. OK, the football was a step up from what we were playing at Raheny United, but in terms of gelling with the girls and feeling welcome it was the same as being in Ireland. That made it a lot easier to decide to make the move.

The trial itself actually wasn't great for me. I don't think I played particularly well. It was against a boys' team but the club maintained that they were still interested in signing me. It was only a couple of days over there and back home again. Then they sent over a contract, I signed it and packed my bags a week later to begin my professional career.

This was in 2015. I had two spells at Glasgow and each represented a new start with professional football. Naturally, I was better equipped for the demands of it the second time round but I had to experience it all first and that is why I jumped at the opportunity to join Scotland's most successful club in women's football.

I couldn't wait to get started that first time. In hindsight, I wasn't ready for that new start though. I had been to Pieta House earlier that year and probably still hadn't dealt with everything that I needed to. In a way, the move to Glasgow was an opportunity for me to run away from my problems, as if a new environment would allow me to start over. Except it didn't as I started to experience panic attacks from very early on in Glasgow.

Looking back on it now, I was so excited – probably a little too excited – to get started. I should have given myself more time to get prepared for it. I didn't know how to control my panic attacks and when they started happening at training it became a very visible thing. Not the greatest thing for your new team-mates to witness!

Everything happened very quickly. After a little while I was in a relationship with a girl on the team and she helped quite a lot with dealing with the attacks. But there always seemed to be a problem. Even in the week leading up to the Scottish Cup Final, in November, I had a urine infection and there were questions about whether I could play. Of course, I put everything to one side, made a brave face and played. And I scored a hat-trick!

On the outside, people remarked that I was flying high but little did they know that I was struggling badly with my anxiety. My brother had come over to watch the final and afterwards we were back in my apartment getting ready to go on a night out to celebrate. I actually didn't feel well and wanted to stay in, but I was persuaded to have a drink and to get ready and the next thing I knew I was out in the city centre. Now, it didn't take much persuasion considering I was known to be a bit of a party girl.

That night, however, just led to a lot more drinking because I then flew home to Cork for the Christmas period and it turned out to be a hectic period that involved drinking almost every day.

It was around that time that I started to question my own self-worth. I was conscious of having to return to Glasgow in shape but I wasn't looking after myself at all. I was eating whatever I wanted, so I put on a lot of weight. This is the opposite to how a professional footballer should be behaving and I knew it. The lifestyle that I was living had no plan, no strategy, I was just hoping that I would wake up one day and everything would be OK. Of course, I wasn't doing anything to help that come about.

It's crazy to think how things had spiralled out of control so quickly. I get given this golden opportunity to kickstart my professional career at a really good club, I score a hat-trick in a cup final and go home for the Christmas break seemingly on the cusp of taking advantage of it all. Except I was drinking and eating crap and dreading the thought of returning to the club to face up to it all.

I only had myself to blame. When I first moved over to Glasgow, I was living with Denise O'Sullivan and she was brilliant for me. In many ways, I couldn't have had a better person than Denise to show me the ropes. She was like an older sister and someone who I really admired for the level of discipline that she has. I had played with Denise at underage level in Cork and with Ireland at international level, so we had a good connection and that helped massively in the early part of me moving to Glasgow.

Denise took me under her wing in a way. She taught me how to cook, clean and how to be prepared as a footballer. She was so dedicated to being the best that she could be and that made me want to work harder. For the first six months that I lived with her, Denise was absolutely brilliant for me. Then she got her move to Houston Dash in the United States. That showed me where football can take you once you work hard.

Instead, I went completely the other way. I wasn't independent or mature enough to do the right things. I was very easily influenced and then when I had the flat to myself I could do what I wanted and invite whoever I wanted over. There were no boundaries or limits and I took full advantage of that. When Denise moved out, two more Irish girls moved in – Keeva Keenan and Savannah McCarthy. We got on great but I was a really bad influence for them. This was their first professional contract and there I was getting them to go out and go drinking.

When you are a younger player you tend to just go with the flow, as if the older player is showing you how things are done. Except I was doing them a disservice. That is something that I think about a lot, the influence that I had on people around me. At

103

that time I didn't care about anything. Moving away and playing football professionally just allowed me to have a different kind of social life. It's an easy trap to fall into when you first move away because you are trying to adapt to a new environment and make new friends. I completely went with it and it brought me down a rabbit hole.

At one stage, Laura Montgomery and Carol Anne Stewart, who ran the club, came to me basically telling me to get my shit together. They said that my apartment had a reputation for being the 'party flat' and that that wasn't acceptable. I should have been paying attention but it was going in one ear and out the other. Quite honestly, I was acting very selfishly and I was getting away with it because I was still scoring goals in games.

One of the things that I couldn't take a short-cut on was the football. The standard in our training sessions and games was really high. Denise was there when I first arrived and you just look at what she has done with her career to appreciate how good she actually is. We also had players such as Leanne Ross, Jo Love, Lee Alexander, Hayley Lauder, Leanne Crichton and Erin Cuthbert, so there was always a very good standard of player at the club.

My introduction to football at that level was quite intimidating. There was a lot of shouting aimed in my direction in those early days and I was nervous at times, but you have to find a way to adapt. I listened to the coaches, watched the other players and trusted in my own ability. Over time I started to feel comfortable among those players because I felt like I had something to contribute to the team.

What I learned is that you only become a professional when you live like a professional on a daily basis. Leanne Ross made that known on the training pitch and I'm thankful she did. But away from the pitch, it is about eating the right food at the right times, drinking plenty of water, getting the required amount of sleep and doing extra work in the gym. Those are the basic needs of a professional footballer and at the beginning I ticked one, maybe two of those boxes. I thought that my talent was enough to get by and it was in a way as I still scored 17 goals in my first season.

The lack of self-discipline was never going to last though. Glasgow manager Scott Booth wouldn't allow it, the senior players wouldn't accept it and my own body couldn't cope with the demands of professional football. When I look back at photos of me during that period I wonder how anyone even let me go on to the pitch. I was miles away from being in the shape that I should have been in. But somehow I got through it.

The club were incredibly supportive throughout and even helped set me up living with a family at one stage. The idea was that being in a homely environment would help me settle down and end my wild ways. It worked, for a short period of time. But after a while I craved to have my own space again and almost felt trapped in that world. I'm someone who likes to be on their own a lot, so my anxiety would start up whenever I felt like too much was happening around me or expected of me.

Football-wise, it was a challenge. We played Chelsea in the knockout phase of the UEFA Women's Champions League and that was a real eye-opener to the level that they were at. Chelsea were packed with star players such as Fran Kirby, Eniola Aluko, Ana Borges, Millie Bright, Drew Spence, Ji So-yun and Niamh Fahey. I had played in the Champions League the year before with Raheny United but this was a different level altogether.

I think that two-legged tie against Chelsea showed everyone at the club what was required in order to advance in Europe. The next year we came up against Swedish side Eskilstuna United, who had Irish international Louise Quinn as their captain, and that was another lesson in being punished for any errors that you make in a game. We were learning all of the time and it would eventually lead to the club reaching the quarter-finals of the competition a couple of years later.

In fact, my best football – or at least my most enjoyable period – was when I re-joined Glasgow in 2019. My first spell started in 2015 and lasted for the guts of two years as I returned home, played with Cork City for a while and then fell out of football. Eventually I got myself back on track and Glasgow came calling again in 2019. I was much more ready for the professional environment that time.

Actually, that period in 2019 was probably my happiest in professional football. We had a ton of hugely important games squeezed into a small window and that made it all the more exciting. It started with the UEFA Women's Champions League and a gripping two-legged tie with Danish side Brøndby.

We won the first leg of that last-16 tie 2-0 but then managed to lose the second game by the same scoreline. That meant extra time was required but nobody could score so it went to a penalty shoot-out, where our 'Super Keeper' Lee Alexander made three big saves.

It was like we had won the Champions League having come through that as we had qualified for the quarter-finals for just the second time in the club's history. Little did we know at the time that our next game, against VfL Wolfsburg, would not take place until a year later due to postponements because of COVID-19.

We didn't have much time to savour that triumph over Brøndby because we were straight back into league action and secured a title soon after.

We were champions again! But, there was still more work to do with the Scottish Women's Cup Final to play.

Up against Hibernian, we were desperate to win this one. It wasn't so much to clinch the domestic double – even though that was definitely a motivating factor – it was more about ending a long wait to lift the cup. Glasgow hadn't won it since my first season back in 2015. Some people joked that they needed me to have a similar impact considering I scored a hat-trick the last time out.

It turned out to be a strange game. Our team was physically exhausted from the previous weeks, so it was our attitude as much as anything that kept us in it. Hibernian scored and then we got two back before half-time. But they came storming back with two more goals to retake the lead. We were really starting to feel the strain but there was no way that we were going to give in.

On 70 minutes, I scored to bring the game level again. Suddenly we had hope again. The clock was ticking down and the last thing we needed was extra time. Then, out of nowhere, the game produced one of those truly wonderful moments where instinct, skill, timing and power combined to win us the game. And I was the one who provided it.

Having pulled wide towards the right wing, I raced on to a long pass, dribbled into the Hibernian penalty area with a ball on my right foot. In an effort to shake off the last defender, I shimmied a little, trying to confuse her about which way I was going to turn with the ball. An opening appeared, so I took it by shifting the ball on to my left foot and letting fly with everything I had. Thankfully, the ball smashed into the top corner of the net. GOOOOALLLLL!!!

You never lose that euphoric feeling when you score a goal. But scoring a last-minute winner in a cup final is simply out of this world. I remember being mauled by my team-mates in the celebration afterwards. Then both Hayley Lauder and Jo Love collapsed to the ground once the full-time whistle blew and I remember Hayley thanking me for ensuring that she didn't have to play extra time.

The photos from that day might me smile so much. It was the first time that I celebrated winning something by being sober, so that was a little odd. But that period was so enjoyable. I still watch the highlights from the Brøndby game back quite a lot.

Believe me, I know how lucky I am for a club of Glasgow's stature to have given me a second chance. I've known a lot of girls in Ireland who never got the break into professional football when they more than deserved to get a shot at it. Football can be cruel like that. It can also be kind, as I discovered by Glasgow standing by me.

Unfortunately, I made a mess of it first time round. The cup final, the Champions League and the freedom of living on my own in a new city did little to satisfy me. I wanted the social life to be more prevalent because that was when I was able to hide the mental health issues that I chose not to address.

When we won, it was all 'Glory, Glory Glasgow City' but the celebrations never lasted. It was like putting on fake tan. You know that it will fade away and bring back your pasty skin tone but you still revel in the time that it makes you look good. I was drinking more and losing the motivation to stay fit. After my first season with Glasgow, I was in a downward spiral and I only had myself to blame.

7

Hometown Blues

THERE'S no place like home. Except that isn't always a good thing. Slipping into a comfort zone can sometimes be the last thing that you need at a particular point in your life. After two seasons with Glasgow City, I'd had enough. I wanted more freedom and less responsibility. I wanted to drink whenever I wanted to and to go on a night out whenever I could. So returning home at the end of 2016 gave me that escape.

My contract had expired with Glasgow but they were keen for me to sign an extension. The only problem was that my behaviour away from the pitch was atrocious. At the end of my second season, I went on a holiday to Thailand and, well, things got a little crazy as I let loose. After one particularly wild night, which included a combination of cocktails, beaches and skinny-dipping, I was brought crashing back to reality when the club sent me a text message to berate me over my lack of professionalism. It turns out someone had made them aware of photos that didn't show me in a particularly good light.

Laura Montgomery let me know that the club was less than impressed with my behaviour. I didn't give a toss though. I responded like a spoilt brat and chose to view Glasgow as the fun police denying me the good time that I deserved.

The club wanted me back in Scotland straight after the holiday but I went home to Cork instead. I never even went back to collect my things, I just gave up on Glasgow. That isn't something I'm proud of because a lot of people at the club went out of their way to treat me well and give me an opportunity to succeed in my career. My mindset, however, was on partying and running away from it all.

Back home, my parents wanted me to feel comfortable so they trusted me to make the right decision. They knew that there was no point in forcing me to go back to Glasgow because my heart wasn't in it. I promised them that I would look for a job and keep myself active. Time at home was what I convinced myself I needed more than anything.

In a way, I was using football as an excuse for my bad behaviour when in fact it had been the one thing that had been keeping me away from a downward spiral. I didn't appreciate what Glasgow had done for me but when you are in such a selfish, immature state of mind those bigger questions don't mean as much to you. All I was focused on was getting my social life back on track, as if the city of Cork had missed my presence on nights out.

I did apply for a few jobs but then a situation fell into place whereby my older sister, Ellen, needed help with the babysitting of her newborn daughter Emily, and was able to give me a few quid for it. Little did I know at the time that this tiny little being with her tiny fingers and toes would become one of the best things to ever come into my life. From day one I adored my niece and that affection only grew stronger once I started looking after her every day.

Yes, I can see the irony of me – someone whose life was all over the place – being charged with the care of a newborn. But it somehow worked and she brought so much happiness to my life. It also gave me some responsibility, which I needed more than I thought I did.

It was around this time that I made a return to camogie. I had met the manager one night and he invited me up to training, while Gemma O'Connor also texted me once she heard that I was back home.

It was flattering to be wanted by the Cork county team, especially since I hadn't played in a few years. And typical of my carefree attitude at the time, I waltzed up to training thinking that I would slip back in as if no effort was required. But a reminder of tough training sessions was about to hit me like a left jab from Katie Taylor.

It wasn't as if the Cork team welcomed me back with open arms. I can remember some of the players being quite cold towards me, as if they were thinking, 'What the hell is she doing here?' And they had every reason to be sceptical. I hadn't played the sport in a few years, I wasn't playing for my local club and I was clearly out of shape. Not to worry, a couple of training sessions would determine how committed I was.

The running track around University College Cork felt like one of those Tough Mudder obstacle courses. All we had to do was complete a few laps, but I pulled out after one, citing a bad back. This wasn't for me, I'm not Sonia O'Sullivan training for the bloody Olympics. Besides which, this was getting in the way of valuable drinking time. Yes, even on that track with some of the best camogie players of all time pushing themselves, all I could think about was getting to the pub for a drink.

I stuck it out for another few weeks, an impostor pretending that I was on the verge of turning my life around at any minute. I played at full-forward in a couple of games but never truly felt comfortable and I knew that my team-mates were whispering that it was only a matter of time before I returned to football full-time. They were right too.

Colin Bell had selected me for the Ireland squad for the Cyprus Cup tournament. Colin was the new Ireland manager and it was clear from the beginning that he was going to shake things up. He had come from the Frauen-Bundesliga in Germany, where he led Frankfurt to glory in the UEFA Women's Champions League. Originally from England, Colin had played and coached in Germany for so long that he brought a lot of their traits to his style of management.

He knew that I wasn't fit but he thought that it would be a good experience for me to be involved. Perhaps he was hoping for it to act as some sort of life-altering week, where I confessed my sins and started the fight for forgiveness. That, sadly, wasn't about to happen anytime soon.

My time with Cork's camogie team, my great comeback, fizzled out. My priority was my social life but I was trying to stick with sport because I didn't want to lose my identity. In my mind, sport was the one thing that everyone knew me by and I didn't want to lose that – even if I didn't want to work hard to maintain it. I ended up walking away from camogie, no big goodbye, nobody trying to convince me to stay and no tears shed. They wouldn't miss me as they would go on to compete in the All-Ireland Final later that year.

On the footballing side of things, we had just come back from the Cyprus Cup and should have been preparing for a friendly game against Slovakia but the senior players decided this was the best time to make a stand. They had been in negotiations with the FAI, with the Professional Footballers' Association of Ireland (PFAI) acting as their representatives, when everything broke down. It became obvious that the FAI were no longer willing to deal with the PFAI and even a mediator could not solve that. The only solution, players felt, was to publicly express our disappointment with the governing body.

There were several key issues on the agenda, such as non-professional players being compensated for loss of earnings when in international camps, access to a nutritionist and gym membership, match fees and bonuses, more home-based training sessions and gear provided before players meet up for camps. They didn't seem like unreasonable things to ask for, especially when everyone knew that the Ireland men's team were treated like royalty compared to us.

While I hadn't been involved with the senior team that long, I knew from my experience at underage level that things were not as professional as they should be for an international team. One of the main things for us was the hand-me-down jerseys and tracksuits. We were never given new gear, it was always second-hand stuff from the senior team, which was often too big and the zips were all broken so you couldn't even close your jacket. It's shocking to think that that was the norm but it needed someone to stand up and say that it wasn't good enough. That someone was Emma Byrne.

Emma was our captain and, for a long time, one of our best players. She had been at Arsenal and witnessed the changing of standards in women's football. I remember during the Cyprus Cup, she called all of the players together to explain the rationale behind it all and why it was important that we stuck together as a team.

I remember Colin Bell wasn't happy with the timing of it all. He wanted us in camp and to focus on playing against Slovakia, but the momentum behind this started to crank up. And once the FAI made it clear that they would no longer meet with the PFAI, a press conference was arranged for Liberty Hall. A lot of it was a blur for me with flashing camera lights, tons of journalists squeezed into a tight room and the PFAI and SIPTU officials leading the way. I just followed the girls and kept quiet; I was there to support the cause but it was the role of the senior players to speak out.

During the press conference, there were some people sitting at a long table and the rest of us standing at the back. I was behind Emma, who was at the centre of it all. She was unbelievable that day, so articulate in how she spoke and she acted like a real leader. As captain she never shied away from anything but that day she went above and beyond for that team.

That was a real turning point in women's football in Ireland and Emma deserves huge credit for leading it. I think Katie McCabe, who was also one of the players there that day, took a lot from how Emma was as a captain and that probably helped her a few years later when she led the team's negotiations with the FAI for equal pay. That proved to be another magnificent achievement and helped to bring women's football forward again.

So much has changed since then and it needed to, from changing in toilets to give a tracksuit back to earning equal pay with the men's senior team, it is unreal to see that transformation. It makes you optimistic for the future and a little envious of the younger players coming through now with access to more home-based training sessions, elite coaching, top-class administrative support and no excuses to distract them from focusing on the football.

I wouldn't play for Ireland again under Colin Bell as my football career started to hit a skid. Sure, I was back playing with my hometown club Cork City in the Women's National League, but my real efforts were being put into my social life. It started to get silly.

As per my regular routine, I would go on a night out and stay out. When I was younger I could

SCORING GOALS IN THE DARK

get away with that but during this period I had the responsibility of looking after my niece. Poor Emily didn't know what was going on. One day I'm there doting after her, the next I'm nowhere to be found, out drunk somewhere. It caused a lot of friction in my house because my brother would have to come home from college to look after Emily as my parents were out working and my sister didn't know what to do.

My mission was pretty straightforward: have a good time for as long as you can. I had no career plan, no life goals. It was all about the next drink. Sometimes that was a night out with friends, sometimes it was just a few pints in the local pub, it didn't really matter. My friends didn't pay too much attention to it because I don't think they knew just how much it had taken over my life.

I would turn up anywhere a party was on. I even gatecrashed the Cork camogies' teams night when they went to the All-Ireland Final. Forget about being invited, I knew people in that room and I was determined to have a good time. It also didn't matter that my real reason for being in Dublin that day was to attend an Ireland home-based training session. Sure, what was more important? The drink was, of course.

One of the players, Amy O'Connor – who was a long-time friend – was staring at me as if to say, 'What's happened to you?' That was quite humiliating and still to this day sends a chill up my spine at the embarrassment of it.

Naturally, I don't remember much of that banquet as I drank so much it was as if I was trying to break a Guinness world record for the amount of alcohol one person could consume in a single night. I'm pretty sure the Cork girls were not one bit impressed with me.

The next morning I woke up and started to panic. I had no mobile phone, no money and no clue how to get home. I was hungover and wandering around Dublin with real fear setting in. My parents had no clue where I was, my friend Amanda was disgusted because I failed to attend Ireland training and the Cork squad had already set off on the road back to the Rebel County. I was lost, confused and terrified.

At some stage, I ended up beside the River Liffey, peering over the edge and crying. I had lost all control of my emotions as I had never felt this helpless before. A woman noticed and came over to ask if she could help. I just let it all out, told her my predicament and that I didn't want to be here anymore. I'm not sure why I put all of my trust in a stranger but she turned out to be something akin to a guardian angel as she brought me to a bus stop and paid for my fare back to Cork.

Once back in Cork, I got a taxi home and my parents were in the kitchen. My mum firstly asked

Winner, Winner: I've been lucky enough to enjoy a lot of success with Glasgow City, including four Scottish Women's Premiership titles

Family Affair: My parents have always been my biggest supporters and it is fantastic whenever they get to come see me play

BFF: I'm not sure where I would be without Amanda Budden. No doubt she is my best friend and I owe her so much

Lowest Point: I took this selfie when admitted to hospital in 2020 in an attempt to reassure people that I was okay. For so long I regretted the photo but now I feel it's important as part of my story

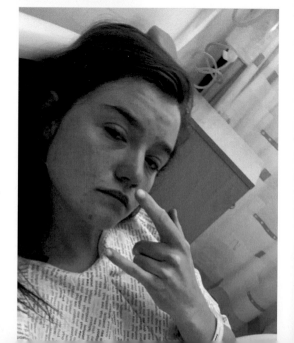

Always by my side: Since my early days in Ireland underage squads I have always been close with Grace Moloney and she remains a great friend

Double Trouble: I've made a lot of friends in football and Leanne Crichton is definitely one who stands out. She has gone above and beyond during my time at Glasgow City

Standing Tall: If it wasn't for the unwavering support of my brother Philip I would never have found the bravery to accept that I had a problem with drugs & alcohol

The Shine Girls: My sister Ellen and my niece Emily always bring a smile to my face. I cherish every second that I get to spend with them

Long Road Ahead: This is when I decided to speak out publicly about my struggles with mental health. It was raining in the Phoenix Park but the photos turned out well

Room-mates, Team-mates: Together with Katie McCabe in Montenegro after returning to the Ireland WNT squad

The Journey Continues: Making my first start for Ireland WNT in our win away to Montenegro in 2020

Ready To Go: Happy times in Ireland WNT camp ahead of our international friendly against Australia in August 2021

Still Fighting: Competing to win possession for Glasgow City in a win over rivals Celtic in the Scottish Women's Premiership in 2022

Bright Future: After all I've been through in recent years, I finally feel happy and I'm looking forward to what is to come — on and off the pitch

where I had been and then ran to me, gave me a big hug and admitted that they were about to file a missing person's report with the Gardaí. It had been over 24 hours since they had heard from me. I was never so happy to see my parents at that moment and I vowed to change my ways so I would never get into that position again.

Unfortunately, I had zero willpower to maintain any sort of disciplined lifestyle. In fact, nothing really improved as I continued to drink and my fitness levels didn't change despite playing regularly for Cork City. Football came easy to me and I was getting away with it.

Ironically, I scored ten league goals that season, plus another six in the cup competitions. I'm not really sure how I managed that return because when I look back at photos of me during that period it's clear that I was nowhere near the kind of shape that I should have been in. At the time I wasn't giving much thought to it because the goals were going in and nobody was complaining.

Certainly, there was nothing but praise shared around when we reached the FAI Women's Cup Final. All of a sudden we were preparing for the biggest game in the women's football calendar and a trip to the Aviva Stadium. It almost felt like I had cheated on my entrance exam and I wasn't about to do anything that would blow my cover. It was a case of keep the head down and make the most of the experience.

In the final we were up against UCD Waves, who had some excellent players including my close friend Chloe Mustaki. But there was no room for sentiment, we had to focus on the game itself. We could have been easily distracted by a lot of factors, such as playing in a big stadium, competing in our first ever final in that competition and that the Cork men's team were on after us as part of a double bill. But we were confident that we could win.

I actually treated that final seriously. My usual intake of alcohol was three or four nights a week, but once we had that date for the final I stayed off the drink for three weeks and I felt that it was my biggest accomplishment yet.

As luck would have it, I got played in behind their defence just past the half-hour mark, took the ball past their goalkeeper who had rushed off her line and somehow fired it into the back of the net with my left foot. It all happened so quickly, all instinct and adrenaline.

That proved to be the only goal of the game, so we went off to celebrate as the men's team took care of their own business. Back in Cork, we were alongside the men's players as part of a double homecoming and the drinking lasted for several months. This was my time to shine, whatever party I was invited to I attended, whatever pub was closest I went inside. It was a great feeling to have scored a winning goal in a cup final and I definitely soaked up all of the attention that came with that.

I was still drinking heavily when, a few weeks later, I travelled with friends to the Netherlands to watch Ireland play in a UEFA European Championship qualifier. That was the famous 0-0 draw and the day when I exposed my drunken state to the Irish team. I was in a tailspin fuelled by consuming alcohol almost every day and it was getting worse.

8

Oh, What a Year

IF I could go back in a time machine, I'd fix the date to 1 January 2018. Then I would set about sidestepping all of the obstacles that previously tripped me up and made 2018 my worst year yet.

Perhaps I should have seen the warning signs flashing as the Christmas period in 2017 descended into chaos because I was drinking more than ever before. It wasn't that I had given up on life, it was that I didn't give a shit about it. All that mattered was chasing that high and escaping from my everyday reality.

Football was still there, albeit barely. I was playing for Cork City but not really trying. If I was at any club other than my hometown team I would have been kindly asked to leave quite a while before.

I was the worst player in training every week, my fitness levels were shocking and my performances on the pitch were embarrassing. But I was getting away with it, or at least I thought I was.

Little did I know that everything would start to come crashing down. This would be the year of my first suicide attempt, of starting in a drug and alcohol rehabilitation centre, of damaging long-term relationships, of being cautioned for possession of drugs and brought to court, of walking away from football and of turning up to international fixtures not even knowing my own name.

It started in January with severe stomach problems that I couldn't explain. Sure, my diet was terrible and I was drinking a lot, but never before did that lead to physical issues. I guess I was just getting away with it up until that point. I knew something was serious when I started bleeding – through both sides – every time that I went to the toilet.

Then the coughing started and it wouldn't go away. I was smoking cigarettes and cannabis, but this cough was constant and I began to worry. The doctor described it as a '100-a-day cough' but it wasn't quite clear what was causing it. I felt terrible and my breathing, especially at night, kept me awake. That was when the cannabis became a regular thing.

Anyone else would have reacted to those issues by getting medical help. Me? I simply partied on. After all, I had built up a reputation by that stage as being the first point of contact if anyone wanted a drinking companion – whether that was for a few too many down the local pub or out on the town.

Eventually, the excessive drinking caught up with me in a way that I didn't expect: a friend sought for help on my behalf. Except I didn't ask for it. Amanda Budden intervened because she didn't know what to do any more about my wild behaviour and deteriorating health. That's what a true friend should do and it's also the kind of selfless act that you would expect of a team-mate in a sporting environment, which is ironic considering that is where it happened.

It wasn't just alcohol that was the problem, I had also developed a taste for cocaine. This new addiction left me in debt and in a really dark place. It was very isolating because you can be sociable when drinking, but not when taking drugs. There were certain people who I would be in touch with just for that. Once my friends clicked that this was the route that I was going down, they didn't want anything to do with it.

On one particular night, I was out drinking and then went in search of drugs. I'm not sure who I was with but I remember waking up the next day in a strange house. I knew the couple who lived there and would have been friendly with them but they were not my friends. I went downstairs and they were having breakfast but I quickly realised that I wasn't meant to be there because I had a game to play for Cork City. Looking at my phone, I had multiple missed calls from my mum, wondering where I was and whether I would be meeting for this game in an hour.

When she arrived ten minutes later she was furious with me. But typical of her she had my kit and gear bag ready. As mad as she was, she couldn't fight the instinct of being a mother and looking out for me. We scrambled to get across to Cork Institute of Technology and I had to get changed in the car.

Unfortunately, I was still intoxicated from the night before so even putting a pair of socks on was an almighty task.

Once we arrived at the ground, I stumbled towards the dressing room, struggling to get the strap of my gear bag to swing over my shoulder. I was a mess. I stepped inside of the dressing room and once I heard the loud music I automatically started to two-step. Quite quickly, the smell of drink lingering from my pores stuffed up the room. That is when a few people realised that I had broken a promise of not going out the night before.

The younger players kept their heads down and tried not to make eye contact. The more senior players pouted in my direction and made it clear that they were ignoring me as I sat there in my Cork City puffa jacket.

Unbeknownst to me, Amanda, who was our goalkeeper and my best friend, stepped outside to inform our manager of the situation. She explained that I needed help, some serious help, and that is when everything started to change.

I didn't play in the game, which was against DLR Waves, so I had to go through it all in this half-drunk, half-embarrassed state. The only thing that lifted my spirits was playing with my niece who had turned up. Unfortunately, Auntie Clare wasn't much use to her that day.

After the game, which we lost, our captain had had enough. Ciara McNamara stood up and just unloaded. At first I tried to brush it off with a joke, but that just infuriated her even more. Normally a soft-spoken girl, Ciara absolutely let rip about how unacceptable this was, how I had let the team and the management down and how I was setting the worst kind of example to young players who looked up to me. Her words hit me like an arrow straight to my heart, bullseye.

What I remember more vividly is that I wasn't invited by my team-mates when they went for a bite to eat after the game. That hurt. The football was one thing, but if I can't even join them in a social setting then something is seriously wrong.

At training, the next Tuesday, I pulled everyone into the dressing room and apologised for my behaviour. I then spoke with the manager, Frank Kelleher, admitting that I needed help and we agreed to start putting a plan in motion. It would be the beginning of my fight against drink and drugs, but also the end of my time playing for Cork City.

Never would I have thought that football was the thing that I would sacrifice first. The game that I had been playing since I was kid was no longer fun. It was more than that though. I think I felt an unease being around my team-mates having disgraced myself in front of them. Repairing relationships and getting people to view you in a better light is not easy, so maybe I just gave up trying on that front.

It was mad to think that I was a professional footballer playing in the UEFA Women's Champions League not too long before all of this. My career should have been on the rise, but instead I was stuck in a vicious cycle that I needed to seize control of. Football didn't reject me, I turned my back on it. And with that went all of the good things in my life – the friendships, the laughter, the challenge of sport, the bit of exercise that I needed and the sense that I belonged somewhere.

Whenever things got difficult at home, Mum would often say, 'I don't know what else to do with you, maybe they can do something about it.' She was referring to the football. As a punishment, no matter what state I was in, she would make me go to football. Maybe I would humiliate myself there and it would open my eyes to what was really going on, or maybe the football would bring out the best in me.

I was still in my early 20s but, for now, football was put to one side. In its place, I joined a new type of club: the drug and alcohol rehabilitation centre. It was set up through Cork City and I was mortified going there for the first time. The centre was in the middle of Douglas so I didn't want anyone to spot me going in, but I knew that I had to go through with it.

Once inside, I met Andrew Fiddow for the first time and he brought me into a room so I could explain why exactly I needed their help. Well, I just let loose and let it all come out. The conversation went on for quite a while as I cried and cried, admitting that I had problems with drink, drugs and mental health. This was one of the most personal experiences that I ever had and it was with a stranger. I guess I needed to let it pour out of me.

Perhaps the best way to describe Andrew is that he was like my personal sponsor. He would be the one I would develop an understanding with, who would advise me along the way and who would act as my rock whenever times got bad. He was a quiet Welshman, but we clicked instantly because he wasn't someone who told me what I wanted to hear, he was the person who told me what I needed to hear.

It wasn't long before I knew that I was a binge drinker. I could go out on a Thursday and I wouldn't stop until the early hours of Sunday morning. Andrew had classed me as someone who didn't know how to stop drinking and that was something we went through in all of its gory detail when our sessions started in July.

But by October I was back drinking heavily, missing appointments and heading towards a crash. That was when everything built towards my first suicide attempt and it was only after that had occurred that I reached back out to Andrew to start over.

So let's take a moment to recap everything. This year, my worst year yet, started with serious concerns over my health, led to my footballing career being paused, entry to a drug and alcohol rehabilitation centre, being reprimanded by a Gardaí for possession of drugs at a concert, facing the possibility of stern outcome from the courts, damaging relationships with close friends and then stepping out in front of live traffic in an effort to kill myself. Could things get any worse?

The failed suicide attempt proved to be the true catalyst for real change. I had a false start earlier in the year but now I was ready to fully commit to it. And I wouldn't have been able to do that without the support of Amanda. She went above and beyond to stick by me.

What was decided, through my sessions with Andrew, was that I needed a lifestyle change and that was through physical activity. Amanda was instrumental in that because it was all well thought out. She had knowledge of nutrition and personal training, so she started by addressing what I was eating. The first goal was to get a better diet. Once that was started, I could add regular training to it. All of a sudden I was putting the right fuel into my body and burning off all of the crap that I collected up to this point.

Amanda and I got into a routine of going to the gym together and that was something that I really looked forward to every day. It's funny looking back at it now because our first day in the gym with a personal trainer was an absolute horror show. Our trainer was asking us what our diets were like and if we drank alcohol. We were laughing to ourselves because I had taken it too far at that stage. I actually weighed more than Amanda even though she was six feet tall and I was five-foot nothing.

We were working for the same company at the time and Amanda would pick me up every day. That was really the start of me getting my shit together because she truly believed in me when nobody else really did. Those days in the car, with the music blaring and us laughing, they were the best days. I had a long way to go but with Amanda's help I made a start with it.

There was a brief scare around the Christmas period when the Gardaí delivered my court summons – for my drug possession earlier in the year – to my house. But I got through it and was able to maintain the productive lifestyle that I had started to establish through my daily interactions with Amanda.

If I could keep this going then there was hope of turning my life around. I may even get back playing football again one day.

The thing that I found most difficult throughout this time was how people viewed me. The stigma around addiction is something that I struggled with. When someone thinks of an alcoholic, they think of someone who is old and homeless. I knew, though, that I still had so much to give – as soon as I got on top of things.

9

Let's Take This Seriously

AS A footballer, there is nothing worse than watching your team-mates out on the pitch when you are unable to take part. No matter the amount of fame or fortune you accumulate in your career, nothing beats the feeling of kicking the ball around with your friends.

It is that sense of inclusion, of togetherness, of team spirit, of combining individual talent with collective grit, of simple fun and of enjoying the beautiful game. No drug can take you higher than that euphoric feeling of being part of a winning team – believe me, I've tried quite a few drugs in my time chasing that artificial high!

I know there will come a day when my body simply won't allow me to play anymore. We all think that we will set new records for competing in sport late into life, but the reality is that we only get so long playing at a high level. I try not to think about the end, but rather focus on what is part of my immediate future. And right now that is all about playing football.

It took a period in isolation for me to appreciate football again. When I say isolation, I mean being left out of the squad by the Ireland manager. I wasn't angry about it because I understood why Colin Bell was overlooking me.

Still, it hurt, but as a footballer, it's important to have that self-awareness of knowing when you deserve it and when you don't.

I went through the self-pity period, followed quickly by the drowning of sorrows downfall and then eventually the 'let's take this seriously' mantra. Those steps to recovery were definitely accelerated by that look Colin gave me in Amsterdam. It wasn't that he tried to show his disappointment, in fact he was probably trying to give a sympathetic smile when he spotted me, but a facial reaction can say a lot about how someone is feeling. I knew that Colin was disappointed in me, why wouldn't he be? I was drunk, overweight and acting like a twat. But it was a sobering moment when he looked at me from a distance.

Even though the motivation to return to the Ireland squad was fuelled by my own desire to succeed, there was also a part of me that wanted to prove to Colin that I was good enough to be involved again. The first part of that was finding a balance in my daily life. It was not too dissimilar from someone starting out on a weight loss challenge or recovering from an addiction, except it was both of those things at the same time. And the very first step must be discovering the self-respect needed to get you through it all.

Reflection is something I have a serious love/ hate relationship with. I love being able to look back over mistakes that I have made and some decisions that lead me straight back to the beginning of a battle I thought that I was in complete control of. Knowing I am not there anymore is a feeling I cannot explain, but sometimes I can't help but hate the realisation of how it all happened. What I have realised is that my past does not define who I am nor does it define where I can go. What it can do is be a guide and a learning curve for me and anybody else who finds that they may be in a similar situation.

You might not have control over everything you want, but you can control your mindset towards it.

People have asked how I got myself out of such a dark place and my reply is always simple: this is my last chance.

I created a small vision that only I could see. It wasn't easy. Actually it was the toughest experience of my life. Every day I woke up feeling like I had failed again. I didn't think it was possible to get everything back on track as I was so riddled with anxiety and had the nagging feeling that it was better just to give up.

I was being controlled by my mind but it wasn't actually being controlled by me. That might be difficult for people to understand and I didn't understand it either.

Every day I woke up, I might not have been all that productive but I still got up, dressed myself and ate some food. Day by day things improved and I added a little bit more each time. I started ticking things off my to-do list.

I set myself a different task and day by day I saw improvements. You know when you feel like things are starting to get better and you are moving past a certain struggle and then one thing changes and you are back to square one? Well that's what recovery is like. It is so up and down. When I talk about recovery, it is through two different points of view: one is just getting myself back in line, the other is the mental and physical recovery process that I've gone through on the back of a near-death experience. This experience, of taking things seriously, very much belongs in that first category.

In order to succeed, you need to adopt the right mentality. There will often be times when it feels like one step forwards and two steps backwards but you have to find that drive to keep going. A good support system always helps because you can't do everything on your own and you should never be afraid to ask for help. The people I had around me have no idea of the positive impact that they had on me. Listen to their words of encouragement, embrace their sense of kindness and be open enough to share with the right people.

Ultimately, you will need to take the necessary steps forward. The best way to do that is to find consistency in a routine. For me that started with an early morning walk or a gym session. Get the blood flowing, release those endorphins and get moving. Then I would arrange a coffee date with a friend or sometimes even go on an unnecessary train journey, so I could embrace where I was and find myself as everyone else rushed by a frantic pace. You set the pace of your life, so don't get stressed by how someone else does things.

I guess I had conceded that my international career was over around that period. Sure, I was back playing with Glasgow and doing OK, but there were other players regularly selected ahead of me and that became a common theme. The Ireland team did quite well under Colin and I envied those who were involved in each international camp.

Then things changed when Colin suddenly left to take up a job with Huddersfield Town and a new Ireland manager was on the way in. Maybe there was still hope for me after all.

Injuries were now my nemesis. A trip to the United States to take on the newly crowned World Cup winners in the summer of 2019 was a missed opportunity, even though a new manager had yet to be appointed. I wanted to be available for when that new person came in to get a fresh crack at resurrecting my international career.

Vera Pauw was the next manager I had to impress. Vera is a legendary figure in women's football, having been capped 89 times for the Netherlands and become the nation's first ever female player to play professionally when she moved to Italy.

She started on her coaching journey very early and has made significant progress with the likes of the Netherlands, South Africa, Russia and Scotland. It was a huge coup for the FAI to be able to bring her in as the new manager.

A new UEFA European Championship qualifying campaign had just started, but it was Tom O'Connor leading the team in the first game at home to Montenegro because Vera's deal had yet to be completed. The girls won that one and then Vera took charge against Ukraine in Dublin. I wasn't involved for either of those, but I was watching closely from afar and hoping to break back into the set-up.

I was playing well for Glasgow and Vera took notice. We had gone on our best ever run in the UEFA Women's Champions League by getting through a group phase before edging past Danish side Brøndby to reach the quarter-finals. There was such a great atmosphere around the club and I felt very much part of it.

The long-awaited call-up to return to the Ireland squad came in November with a qualifier away to Greece. The buzz that I felt was unreal. Of course, typical of my life, nothing was straightforward. I felt a lot of anxiety in that camp, probably putting too much pressure on myself, and then I got injured in a training match in the National Indoor Arena and had to be stretchered off. Thankfully it wasn't too serious and I made the trip to Athens.

Even though I was an unused substitute – I wasn't fit enough to play if being honest – I was just happy to be involved again. We drew the game 1-1, or rather gave it away late on when we conceded. The highs and lows of international football were back and I couldn't get enough of it.

Back in Glasgow, we had a Scottish Cup Final to contend with. Hibernian were our opponents and it proved to be a tough game with each side cancelling each other out once they had scored. I got two goals myself, including the winner in the 90th minute. This was more like it, scoring goals in big games. And it was another winners' medal with Glasgow.

Only a year before I wasn't even playing football and I was in the drug and alcohol rehabilitation centre. So to get back to this stage was unreal. It was the happiest that I had felt in such a long time. And it was my first sober celebration after winning something. It was funny sitting there pouring a Coke Zero into a glass with everyone else in the background absolutely langers (a Cork term for being drunk). That was such a change to be able to control my mindset and how my body felt too. Maybe I could get used to these sober celebrations.

I continued to stay focused over that Christmas period, which I felt was the right time to speak out about my struggles with mental health. Everything in my life was flowing well and I couldn't wait for the next game. As much as it has served as a release from the stress of my everyday life, sometimes football was the last thing that I wanted to do. However, this new approach to taking it seriously was paying off.

Vera called me into the next Ireland squad – a double-header in March 2020 – and I was walking on air, feeling so ready to pull on that green jersey again. First up was Greece at home at the Tallaght Stadium. I was actually quite nervous before the game. Sitting on the bus en route to the stadium, I had my headphones on and was texting my mum. I got quite emotional, thinking of how far I had come to get in this position again.

I was on the bench as a substitute and did my best to stay focused on the game. Every time Vera glanced back towards the bench or there was a long stoppage in play I wondered if I could get the nod to get ready to come on. Eventually that call came on

86 minutes and I replaced Ruesha Littlejohn. My adrenaline was pumping so hard that I thought I was going to burst a blood vessel. We won 1-0 and I went straight into the crowd to hug my family as soon as I got the chance to.

It might have only been a brief cameo at the end of the game, but it showed that Vera was prepared to trust me. She went even further a couple of days later by selecting me in the starting line-up for our game away to Montenegro. Wow. A first senior start for my country. This is what I dreamt about for so long and I felt ready to grasp it.

Montenegro was beautiful. I remember going for a walk one morning with Katie McCabe down the beach front and taking it all in. This is what my life was meant to be like: on international duty, experiencing it with my close friend. After all of the crap that I had been through – all of my own making, admittedly – this was where I wanted to be.

The game against Montenegro kind of passed me by. I was probably overthinking it and I didn't get into the flow of it at all. That's international football though, it can be unforgiving. But I knew that I was ready to test myself at that level. We went on to win the game 3-0 and that put us in a great position to push for qualification to the European Championship finals. As we left Montenegro, everyone was buzzing with the result but also wary of the news that a global pandemic was about to hit via the COVID-19 virus.

I didn't know it at that time but the best run of my career, which included a return to the Ireland squad, a first senior start, a superb run in the Champions League and two goals scored in the Scottish Cup Final, was about to come to a crashing halt.

10

Speaking Out

WHEN you share your vulnerabilities and admit to your mistakes, people gravitate to you as if you have all of the answers to their problems. You can sense when someone approaches you just because they associate you with mental health and that's fine. I've put myself out there and spoken about it so there is no going back.

Part of me enjoys talking about it. Certainly if I can help anyone by telling my story or giving some sort of insight that might work for them then it's very much a positive thing. But there's no turning back now that I've been so public in speaking about my own mental health.

It was something that I had on my mind for ages. This is going back to 2019, after I got into the Ireland squad under Vera Pauw for the first time. I felt that I was in a good place and sharing my story with people could possibly help someone else who might be going through something similar. Except I didn't know how to do that. So I reached out to Gareth Maher, who is the ghost writer on this book, and asked for his advice. He was the media officer with the Ireland women's team and had been there in 2014 with the under-19s when we went to the European Championship in Norway. If anyone was going to know how best to tell my story, I thought it would be him.

Around December 2019, I sent him a message expressing my desire to speak out publicly about my struggles with mental health. In fairness, Gareth said to think about it over the Christmas period and if I still felt as strongly about it then he would help in January.

But my desire to share my story only grew stronger over that Christmas so I reached out again to him in January. By that stage he already had a whole plan put together.

The first step was to set the tone and shape the narrative through my own words. We linked up with The Sports Chronicle, which is a website that allows sports professionals to express themselves in a way that suits them. When you do an interview with a journalist, there is an element of risk involved because you never know how they are going to treat it, what angle they are going to take and what parts of your story they are going to focus on. That's why this platform was a good starting point; it was using my words.

In order to best describe what I was going through and what I wanted to say, I wrote my piece as if it were a letter to my younger self. The 20x20 campaign gave their support to it and that gave it a huge boost, plus a lot more eyeballs. The reaction was very positive but it was only the first part of the plan. Next up was speaking with the media, because you cannot ignore the influence that they can have.

So I flew from Glasgow into Dublin on a Thursday, we got professional photos done by *Sportsfile* in the Phoenix Park, and then we went to the Castleknock Hotel for selected interviews. It was all handled so well. I even had a personal driver, Martin Byrne, for the day and he made me feel at ease because he is such a great character.

In the hotel, I did one-on-one interviews with Liam Mackey of the *Irish Examiner*, Emma Duffy from The42 and Marie Crowe of RTÉ. While I had done plenty of interviews in the past, this time it was

165

different because it was all about my struggles. So yes, a few tears flowed at times but I thought that I handled myself well and said all of the things that I wanted to. I had my notebook in front of me on the table and dipped into that a couple of times. The guys were great too, Liam, Emma and Marie; they were so understanding and the pieces that they produced afterwards were great.

I probably underestimated what sort of reaction that it would have but it was huge. Every newspaper, website, radio station, TV channel carried my story and used the photos that we took. It led to a lot more media requests. It was certainly an eye-opener as to how much my story resonated with people – especially when I saw the reaction on social media and read all of the messages that came through. That was when Gareth and I first spoke about writing this book, as there was so much more that I wanted to share.

Then I had my breakdown in June 2020, only a few months after all of that. In a way it was like going back to square one. For all of the things I spoke about in those interviews, about being disciplined, abiding by a routine, being positive, I simply fell off the wagon. Except this time it was now done in a very public way as I had gone missing following a party in Edinburgh and people raised the alarm to start a search for me. By all accounts, it was trending on Twitter and everyone connected with Irish and Scottish football seemed to know that I was missing. Even the first minister of Scotland, Nicola Sturgeon, tweeted about it. So much for suffering in silence!

Once I was ready I knew that I wanted to speak out again. There was a power to it. Almost therapeutic, it helped me to cope with my own situation but because I had nobody to lean on who had similar experiences that made me even more determined to help others. It's why the idea of the book was resurrected and why I opened up in a video interview with Laura Montgomery in September 2021. Laura, who is CEO at Glasgow City, has been one of my most trusted confidants and I've always been able to relate with her. She lost her partner through suicide and that's why we did the video, to speak openly about that topic and try to break down the taboo nature of discussing it.

What I didn't expect on the back of that video was a feeling that I had let some people down. It's OK for me to tell my story but I realised that when I mentioned other people that it suddenly brought them into the public spotlight, without them necessarily agreeing to it. In the video with Laura, I just spoke honestly and didn't realise at the time that I was making other people part of my story. It was only afterwards, when it was brought to my attention by someone, that what I had said sunk in. It has made me think twice before mentioning anyone in interviews.

One of the things that Laura mentioned during that chat was me being a role model. When I've been at my lowest ebb, I cannot imagine anyone would dare to describe me as a figure that they would look up to. Yet, that is when I'm at my most resilient. That is when I'm truly fighting back, when I'm ignoring that devil on my shoulder, when I'm jumping out of the bed to overcome my anxiety and when I'm not letting all of the good work count for nothing. And that is why I wanted to write this book – to show girls and women that there is someone out there who has been through what they have.

There have been a lot of people who have gone before me and spoken so passionately about mental health. I remember coming across a video of Niall Breslin, where he spoke out about his problems. That really resonated with me because I liked his music but also because he had experienced that weight of expectation as a young sports star. He was tipped by many to become a brilliant rugby player but he struggled with the pressure of it all. I can't tell you how many times I watched that video. It really helped to know that someone had been through similar things and, again, that's why this book was important to do because I don't think there is a single book from a female footballer who has been so open in this way while still playing.

I fully understand that I'm only in this position because of my talent and achievements as a footballer and that is what people will gravitate towards when searching for a role model: the goalscorer, the international footballer. Yet, a true role model is surely someone who shows us all sides of them. Merely presenting your best side is almost a cop out, if you're going to embrace the responsibility of being a role model then go all in.

Of course, I'm not medically qualified to guide someone through their darkest hours or prescribe a remedy that best suits them. But what I can do is share my story and experiences to show that girls and women are not alone in feeling how they do at certain times. And if my openness can have a positive effect on just one person then it was all worthwhile in speaking out.

What I've found extremely powerful is using social media as way to connect with others who are going through tough times. By simply sharing my feelings I can provide a window into my world and show people that it's OK to not be OK at times. The instant reaction from social media and its reach all around the world has opened my eyes to a different way of sharing my experiences.

A good example would be when I came across a post on Twitter from a guy who was sharing his before and after images. The before was when he was drinking and at his lowest point. The after was when he was clean and sober. The transformation was mindblowing and it really made me realise what recovery can do for people.

Little did I know that I played a small part in that man's recovery. I didn't know him at all but he reached out, via a direct message on Twitter, to reveal that my postings of my own struggles inspired him to make a change. There are many pitfalls with using social media but this incident reassured me that it can be a platform for good too. And it proved that telling my story was a positive thing to do.

Of course, there will those who judge me and accuse me of seeking attention but I know why I am doing this and that is what matters most.

11

Relapse

I SPENT 30 days in a psychiatric ward in a mental health hospital in Glasgow. It was my first experience in a place like that. There were 20 patients on completely different journeys and I spent the first 18 days crying.

Some days the Nairn Ward in Stobhill Hospital felt like a cavernous banquet hall that stretched on for miles. On other days, it felt claustrophobic as if the walls were closing in with every passing hour. Your mind can play tricks on you in a place like this, mainly because your mind has been damaged in some capacity hence the reason you being there in the first place.

My first few days were a bit of a blur. It took some time to realise where I was and why I was there. My body was flushing out toxins as my mind tried to find steady ground so that my memory bank could realign with both sides of my brain and stop spinning around. If I was playing a game of Operation, it would be like some of the pieces were missing from the box in order to make up the human brain. The motor area did not fit in snugly beside the sensory area, while the frontal lobe was backwards.

Once I accepted that I was going nowhere in a hurry, I had to come to the terms with how I ended up in a mental health hospital. And, of course, it was all of my own doing. The self-destructive side of me had gone too far and a suicide attempt had left me in this helpless state where I could barely feed myself or muster up the strength to sit upright on the side of the bed. This was not exhaustion, this was being broken – mentally and physically.

Then the guilt started to set in. How am I in this position again? How have I allowed myself to deteriorate like this again? What are people to think? What are people saying about me?

I had been doing so well. After such a turbulent few years, I was eating right, working out regularly, being kind to myself and others, keeping my demons in check and starting to make progress for club and country on the pitch. Then COVID hit and threw my world into a frenzy.

Having just played for Ireland against Montenegro, I flew back to Glasgow as the virus started to spread across the globe. A national lockdown order instantly deprived me of access to a gym, interaction with friends and team-mates, the freedom to get out into the fresh air and explore the world and the consistency of any sort of normal routine. I was trapped inside an apartment and suddenly felt more lonely than ever before in my life.

Everyone I knew had disappeared back to their own homes. Yet here I was in a city that suddenly felt foreign, locked inside for almost 24 hours a day and nothing to do but drink and attend the weekly Zoom family quiz. I tried to prepare myself by buying a jigsaw, PlayStation games as well as a hurley and sliotar, but that all lasted a week before I grew bored of them. The most exciting thing at that stage was my daily trip to the off-licence.

It was like a scene from a movie where the first-time convict gradually starts to lose their mind once that prison door slams shut. A window teases a glimmer of light into the cell, but the door remains shut. That is when the demons come out and begin to cause mischief by telling you how worthless you really are.

The lonely days turned to weeks. Sentenced to rot away in a lifeless apartment, I felt like there was no point any more. No point in eating correctly. No point in exercising. No point in looking ahead to a future that may not exist. I was stranded in an urban dwelling as the world continually reminded us that this new type of existence was going to be around for quite a while. I just couldn't cope with it all.

A brief reprieve came around a month later when I managed to catch a flight home to Cork. At this point there was no mention of PCR tests, it was a case of covering up and hoping for the best. When at home, I started drinking again as I took advantage of my new-found freedom. On that first night, I was with my family in the back garden sharing conversation with our neighbours over a concrete wall. As the evening went on I started to have a few bottles of beer, thinking that it could be managed while in a home environment. But that is typical of the mindset of an alcoholic, tricking themselves into thinking that the next time will be better and that they won't get hooked on it again.

Over the next few days, I started to feel suicidal again. I went to see a doctor and he prescribed anti-depressants, but I felt let down by some of the things he said to me that day. I had just opened up to him yet it was like he didn't believe me. He almost brushed things off by saying, 'I don't want to see your face in a newspaper for the wrong reasons.' It was like he was throwing me a bottle of pills and telling me to be on my way.

I eventually flew back to Glasgow and news filtered through that the Scottish government were finally set to ease restrictions and lockdown would end. I craved the company of others. So when an invite came to join some people at a house party, I jumped at it. But this was the equivalent of a convict being released from prison and going back to their old friends, the ones who corrupted them in the first place, and enjoying a night out. I didn't care, I needed to let loose.

The English Premier League was on TV and I was watching three live games back to back while downing bottles of Corona. The night before, I had given serious thought to committing suicide but managed to talk myself out of it and crashed into bed. The next day I picked up 24 more bottles of beer and then another four cans of Corrs Light to drink in an Uber on the way to Edinburgh where I knew a house party was on.

I remember asking the driver if I could open a bottle for the journey and I played some music while texting friends. By the time I arrived at the house I was stumbling in the door.

The girls were shocked at how drunk I was. They wanted nothing to do with me, to avoid that responsibility of what might happen to me. I felt that there was no point in arguing, so I avoided that and just kept on drinking. At some stage, I managed to get hold of some cocaine from a guy who was there and that kept me wired. No wonder I was the last one to go to sleep.

At eight o'clock the next morning, in Where's Wally pyjamas, I raided the fridge to snatch a bottle of wine, grabbed my bag and left the house. I just walked and walked, which led to a wooded area and then I stopped. The tears were streaming down my face and I started to type what would be my goodbye letter in the Notes app on my phone. This was it, I was coming to the end.

I got up and started walking again. I jumped over a fence and ended up on some farm. I had no clue where I was going but I kept on walking regardless. Then I got on a bus which took me to Prince's Street Gardens. Families were having picnics and it was a really warm day. I got some chips from a food stall and sat next to a lake, sharing some chips with the birds and swigging on the bottle of wine.

Hungover yet still drinking, I could feel the blood beneath my cheeks as the warmth of the sun blazed down from above. The hours ticked by and I drank even more. Even though I was in no state whatsoever to make any kind of decision, I came to the conclusion that this was the end. Time to end this misery and stop letting myself and everybody else down.

Little did I realise that the alarm had been raised that morning with someone declaring that I was missing. The police were on the lookout for a Glasgow City footballer, aged 25, but their search was leading to nothing. What they should have been looking for was a down-and-out drunk who looked like a tramp and was slumped over somewhere near a river.

After around ten hours, they found me. I think someone had spotted me and rang the police. I wasn't aware of it but social media was lighting up about my disappearance. Websites and radio stations reported about it, urging people to keep an eye out. And almost everyone connected with women's football in Scotland and Ireland shared posts across their channels.

I was taken directly to hospital where they had to pump my stomach, get fresh fluids into me and ensure that I didn't choke on my own sick. I drifted in and out of consciousness, just enough to post a photo on Twitter of myself from the hospital bed saying, 'Thank you everyone, I'm struggling and that's OK. I'll be back. Look after yourself.'

The photo isn't pretty. My face is swollen, my eyes are heavy, my hair is raggedy, my skin is off colour and my expression screams of helplessness. I wish that photo didn't exist. But I'm learning, day by day, that you cannot hide away from your past. You have to accept the decisions that you made and move on accordingly. My time in recovery in hospital helped me come to terms with that.

To view Stobhill Hospital from the outside, it could be mistaken for a modern school or even a fancy office space. Perhaps what gives it away as being a hospital is the giant clock tower that has clearly weathered many a storm through the years. The sight of the red-brick tower with a clock face on each of its four sides reminds us that we are all on borrowed time.

Originally built in 1901, Stobhill catered for military casualties from the First World War who arrived via a special train that stopped on the hospital grounds. Over the years, it expanded to include a radiology department and maternity unit before the NHS took control after the Second World War. It has since advanced with an upgrade in 2009 at the cost of £100m and a fancy-looking exterior added. Nowadays it serves the community of North Glasgow for specialist services with the accident and emergency department gone along with the maternity unit. It is a special hospital for special patients.

I'm not sure if special is the right word. In school, if I was selected as the special student I would receive a gold star from the teacher. There is no such adulation shared in this old building. This is where serious truths are spoken and where the real pain cannot be seen.

Stobhill was not somewhere I wanted to be. In the first few days I was angry that someone had put me here. Afraid to accept that I needed this rehab more than anything I have ever known, I still knew that it wasn't right for someone in their 20s to be in this situation.

Riddled with anxiety, I was trying out different medication to see which ones worked for me. My period was very up and down. My stomach swirled like a washing machine, rejecting some drugs and accepting others. Between hallucinations, nightmares and completely forgetting who I was and what my purpose was, I stumbled through each day as if trying to figure out a puzzle.

Lying in bed at night, I heard the alarm going off again and again as patients attempted to escape. Every morning I would wake up and plot my own plan of action. I thought to myself, 'If I ran they would never catch me,' but in reality if I was to run 100 metres I would probably have fainted. Where was I going to escape to anyway? I had to accept that this was where I needed to be, this was where I needed to get better.

The other patients in my ward were much older than me. They had lived a lot longer and suffered a lot more. We sparked up friendly conversation and they gave me the kind of advice that only someone with 10 or 20 years of mental health issues can. I think they envied me in a way, believing that I was young enough to still turn my life around. It would take some time before I was able to see it that way but their sharing of their stories helped to fast-track it.

There were some truly remarkable people in the hospital. One old man would occupy the same bench each morning, smoking a cigarette from tip to butt without even a flicker of ash falling away. He was a former soldier and suffered from flashbacks of being in a war zone, so you would constantly hear him yell out about 'taking cover'. Everyone suffered in their own way.

It was a scary place to be at times. The only thing that settled it all down was the distraction of a daily routine. Four meals a day followed by, 'Clare, your meds are ready.' Oh, and how could I forget the Mr Whippy van which arrived twice a day! Anyone who knows me will attest to my love of ice cream, but unfortunately my appetite was nowhere to be seen. As the rest of the ward stuffed themselves with crisps, chocolate and fizzy drinks, I sat in silence as everything around me felt so loud.

My love and respect for the nurses grew every day. They really were amazing and they believed in me when I didn't believe in myself. My daily walk to the front desk consisted of me burying my chin into my chest to avoid eye contact with anyone as tears flowed in a steady stream down my face. I didn't utter a word. Yet they knew that I needed to let off some steam. Entering into a room with such uncertainty and pain, but leaving with more of an understanding of the feeling that I was going through – that became a daily ritual.

I lost all sight of who I was. I couldn't see my life ever going back to the way it was. I doubted myself to the point I didn't want to continue. I was broken into a million pieces and the process of putting me back together would take a lifetime. That feeling is still there, but I'm learning to cope with it.

While stuck inside the hospital, I came to the realisation that life really does go on. Literally everyone I knew in the world got on with their daily lives – working, eating, laughing, crying, sharing things with each other, making plans for the future. The feeling that you are somehow indispensable was burst like bubble. So if you are going to make the most of your life and have a positive impact then you better get going with it while you still have the chance.

Visting the ward was difficult because we were still in the middle of COVID so protocols around the hospital were very strict. Also, the nursing staff want to ease patients back into contact with people so that the recovery process is not upset at all. Of course that didn't stop my brother, my lifelong friend from home, Shannon Dempsey, and my team-mate Leanne Crichton from turning up to see me. They weren't allowed past the front door but it was such a relief to see some friendly faces.

Shannon is someone who has always been there for me. We grew up together, played on the same camogie team and experienced many highs and lows. Yet it was still surprising to see her sitting next to my bed when I woke up the next morning after my breakdown; almost like my guardian angel being there for me. Ironically, Shannon works in the same hospital as a physiotherapist, so she was able to use her access to get on to my ward. True friends go out of their way to be there for you and that is what Shannon has always done. Our friendship is one that will never fade away, no matter what happens.

After a few days, I was allowed to venture beyond the front door. Sam Kerr, a former team-mate, came to see me and we walked around the car park, taking in the fresh air and chatting away. That time was so precious because it reminded me that people truly cared for me. In fact, Sam and Nicola Docherty looked after my things while I was in hospital and I'll be forever grateful to them for their support.

I was always worried about being judged over my behaviours, especially within the football community. But reassurance came through a flying visit from Grace Moloney on one of her off days. Grace and I first met in the Ireland under-17 squad all those years ago and we have always maintained a strong friendship. When she could, she took the first flight from London – she plays for Reading – up to Glasgow. Grace helped to remind me that I was loved.

I needed a plan. How was I going to reconstruct my life? There wasn't a chance that I would be able to go straight back to my club and starting playing again. I had to learn how to walk on my own, step by step. In order to do that, I needed help and that's where my brother Philip stepped up. He has long been the one who I have turned to at my darkest moments as I have always felt that he understood more than others ever could. So he was the ideal person to help me put everything back together.

I'm so thankful to Philip for putting his life on hold to move over to Glasgow and help me get my life restarted. He was there when I woke up in the morning to encourage me to have breakfast. He was there to accompany me on a walk outside. He was there to cook meals, sort out my medication and be the friend that I needed to lean on. Up to that point in my life I was too proud to admit that I needed this kind of help. Don't be stupid like I was, ask for assistance.

It took many months before I felt like myself again. There were times when I wanted to give up but Philip was there throughout it all as my support network. When you relapse, you hit rock bottom. It's a long way back to the top.

12

The Comeback

SOMETIMES I wonder why certain people have afforded me a second, third or fourth chance. I've done more than enough to hurt those closest to me yet they are the ones who still stand by me. I'm lucky, I guess, very lucky.

One of those people was Scott Booth. He is the manager who I have worked under for longer than anyone else and it's fair to say that he knows how to get the best out of me. In two different spells, he trusted me to be a key player for his Glasgow City side and persisted with me in spite of the various distractions that I created along the way.

I definitely tested his patience through the years and I fully understand if he held any reservations about me hitting top form again following my relapse in 2020. Sometimes I think about that, about whether I was deserving of the opportunities that have fallen my way time and again.

The other part of my comeback involved getting back up to speed with the football. That proved to be really tough. In previous years, I had experienced a couple of periods where I had to shed weight to get match fit again and that wasn't easy. But this transition back to playing following my breakdown was totally different.

Leading up to the UEFA Women's Champions League game against VfL Wolfsburg, I turned up to training, mainly to show face and in the hope that it would boost my spirits. I was delicate, weak and vulnerable, which showed up when I tried to make a routine pass to Lee Alexander and I strained my medial ligament. This was a massive indicator that I had a long way still to go and I started to question whether I wanted to pursue with football any more.

It was a horrible feeling being so fragile in front of my team-mates. At that time, I was only able to really eat one meal a day – the first time in my life that I had a difficult relationship with food. The medication that I had been prescribed took over and at times I thought it was making me worse. But as the saying goes, 'It always gets worse before it gets better.'

My biggest fear in life is losing my mind completely. While I was experiencing this attempted comeback that is exactly how I was feeling. It was like my mind was in survival mood. The simple things became incredibly difficult to complete, such as brushing my hair, getting a shower or tying my shoe laces.

With the little energy that I still had, whenever around people, I tried my best to show that I was doing better than I actually was.

All I could do was slow everything down and take it day by day. Do you know how frustrating that is for a professional footballer? This was my job, my livelihood and yet I could only do it in bits and pieces. It was like I had to teach my brain and my body how to connect again whenever I took to the pitch. That was the training pitch because I was a good while away from playing again.

I'll never forget Laura Montgomery sending me a text message to invite me to travel with the Glasgow City squad to Spain for that Champions League game against Wolfsburg. I was taken aback by the gesture and immediately started to feel anxious. How would my team-mates react to seeing me in this way? How would I be able to tailor my new-found routine? It was an evening kick-off and

I had to be in bed for 9.30pm, so that was the first thing to worry about.

Part of me didn't want anyone to see how much of an effect this whole period was having on me. I was putting on a brave face to disguise what I was actually going through. Then again, the other side of me wanted to show my vulnerability as well as the changes that I had made to my everyday life. My routine had become my everything and I couldn't break that. But I wanted everyone close to me to see that I was trying.

I took the leap regardless. In a way it was like my own personal skydive – kicking out my feet and trusting that everything would turn out and I would land OK. Everyone was great with me but my body clock was operating on a different time zone, so when the game eventually ended I was falling asleep in the dressing room and someone had to bring me out to the bus. Even at dinner back at the team hotel, I had to concede that I couldn't socialise any more. I was done for the day even though my team-mates had many hours left ahead of them. This was part of my new routine, though, and it was good for them to see that.

After arriving home from the trip, I met with our strength and conditioning coach Andy White. I explained how I felt the mountain in front of me was too great to climb. My priority, I told him, was to complete my recovery and to find happiness again. Football didn't seem to be part of that. However, he reassured me with the correct steps to help create a mindset that points me in the right direction. He stressed that a positive approach was key to everything else clicking into place, such as regaining my confidence and everything that comes after that is a bonus – which includes football. I had to focus on me before I could even think about football again.

When I did eventually pluck up the courage to walk through the doors of the gym, I was a shell of myself, weighing in at around 56kg. This was a completely different version of me to the one that stumbled up to the gym in Cork with Amanda Budden trying to lose weight all those years ago. This time around I had no muscle mass and for the first two weeks I had to go through the basics of learning how to sit down and get back up. Forget barbells, I was teaching myself how to stand on my own two feet again.

As the weeks went by and probably still to this day I struggled with my breathing and dizziness, while my memory is sometimes nowhere to be found, as if looking for words on a blank sheet of paper. But once I learned to control it then it does become a bit easier. One morning, about four weeks into this process, I took a photo of myself and compared it to when I had first started and WOW, the difference was unbelievable. But the most notable thing from the photo was that I was smiling.

Those first signs of progress led to me believing that it was indeed possible to get back playing football again. Andy was right, I needed to focus on the little things before even attempting to do what came naturally to me in the past.

When I eventually got back involved with the team, it was such an exciting experience. To be back in the dressing room, getting my kit on and being named as one of the substitutes, it felt like I was a kid again doing the thing that I love. We were playing Hibernian in a league game and I got the call with about ten minutes remaining to get ready. Scott Booth said to me, 'You deserve this.' That gave me such a boost and I went on to the pitch to make my comeback.

I found it very hard to understand that a lot of things had now changed, such as previously being able to use my power and body to hold up the ball, but now that I was a lot lighter that had changed. Surprisingly, I never lost my touch and control. My brain did find it difficult to keep up with the pace and intensity of the game, but that was something that I would have to learn to adapt to. Everything around me felt like it was moving at 100 miles per hour.

After a few substitute appearances, I got my first 90 minutes in a horrible 5-0 defeat to Rangers. The adrenaline got me through it but afterwards it was as if my body rejected that extreme high. I had to run to toilet to throw up. Mentally that was one of my first setbacks because all I could think of was that my body wasn't able for such high intensity any more.

Forget about football for a minute, my life did a complete 360-degree turn in the space of six months. I used to be bubbly, outgoing and up for doing things whereas now I was happy in my routine and don't want any distractions.

It was six months after I had been released from hospital that I got to go home for Christmas to see my family. Initially, they didn't know how to react around me. In Ireland, as I'm sure is the case in many countries, the main ingredients around that festive period are chocolate, crisps and alcohol. It was as if my family had to change everything because of me and I didn't want them to feel that way. My life was my responsibility and they had to live their lives.

This was Christmas 2020 and for the first time in as long as I can remember I was excited about what the new year would bring. My recovery was ongoing and there would still be a lot of hard work ahead but I was starting to believe that a brighter future was possible to achieve. A future where I could be happy and realise my ambitions.

There was always a part of me that wanted to let football go. Life, it seemed, would be easier without the demands of football. Although the eight-year-old version of myself never wanted to let it go, she wanted me to continue to play and get back scoring goals again. I had to be honest with myself because even the smallest injury might set me back to square one, so I had to find an inner resolve to truly believe that football could still be in my life.

That was when I realised that there was a lot more to life than football. I could see that I had a lot more to give when before I thought that my true identity was football.

During the first couple of months of 2021, a lockdown was once again imposed due to a spike in COVID-19 cases. This time, though, I was in a much better place to deal with it. Living with my brother was a massive help because he was able to see the positive in every situation.

In April, I changed my medication because it was making me feel sick and I was constantly drowsy. My doctor recommended a lower dosage and that had a big affect on me as suddenly I was unable to understand basic instructions during training drills and I was back in bed for a ten-day stretch. Once again, I started to doubt whether a career as a professional footballer was for me.

Due to these changes, I was ruled out of action for the remainder of our season. In contrast, my team were flying high and would go on to win the league title. That was hard to take because it felt like I had to start my recovery all over again.

This time, though, I was determined to make it work. I wasn't about to give up. So bit by bit, day by day I went through the process of getting myself back to a position where I could return to training in a mental and physical state that allowed me to perform. I started to feel that I was getting back to my old self.

Yet sometimes you can trick yourself into thinking you are ready for something. I certainly did that when Vera Pauw was keen to call me back into the Ireland squad. Except I was ready, in a way, just not to the full extent. Maybe I was operating at 60 per cent capacity when I needed to be fully charged to cope with the demands of international football.

I was called up for the international friendly double-header away to Iceland, but I told Vera that I wasn't quite ready for it. Yes, I turned down an international call-up. Of course I felt guilty and afraid that I might be overlooked for future squads, but it was the right decision at that time. My body was still getting used to the medication that I was on and I needed another couple of weeks to work on my fitness levels. Vera was brilliant about it all and told me to take my time with it. She reassured me that I wouldn't be forgotten about.

One of the big obstacles that I have to deal with each time I take part in international football is the travel. I'm not a good flyer. You would think at this stage, living away from home, that I would be used to it but I'm not. And there is nothing but flight after flight during an international camp – sometimes up to three or four in the space of a few days. My levels of anxiety would be through the roof.

Then there is the routine. Everything in international camps is scheduled from the moment you wake up to when you are going to sleep at the end of the day. It can be difficult to find some time for yourself. But I took that to an extreme when I first returned to the Ireland squad by staying in my room a lot or even if I went to the hotel lobby it was to be on my own with a book. I wasn't really looking to socialise with the other girls, to go for a coffee or a walk or anything like that.

So there were little things, like the travelling, the not mixing with other people, that meant I wasn't doing things right. At the time I thought I was doing fine, but when I came back into the squad again under Vera in the summer of 2021 I had a completely different mindset. I felt that I was in control more than I had ever been before. I know that I'm never going to perfect that and it's something that I've accepted – life goes on, there's no waiting around for anyone.

When my chance to return to the squad did arrive, I felt on top of the world. Honestly, for possibly the first time, I felt like the real me. I was really fit, in good shape and had worked hard in training. A lot of people remarked that I was a different person around the hotel, that it was like having the old Clare back.

The game itself didn't go to my plan as I was an unused substitute when we beat Australia in a friendly at the Tallaght Stadium. I definitely have a better understanding and appreciation for what is demanded at international level.

International camps are incredibly intense. It's 100 miles an hour and there are things happening all of the time. Then when you come out of it, it's like, 'Woah, what do I do now?' You are trying to go back into your old routine and once you're settled into that then there is another international camp coming up in a week or two. That's something that I always struggled with. Stability is something that I need in my life and I get that from having a good routine. Going through recovery you learn a lot of things about yourself and being self-aware is instrumental. Now, I am able to learn a lot more and recognise my triggers.

There is also a mental side of dealing with that adrenaline rush and the demands placed on you. It's something that I've spoken about with our Ireland medical staff, Dr Maeve Doheny and physio Angela Kenneally. They are brilliant and sometimes the best medicine is having a good chat.

Actually, talking about things is something that I'm more comfortable with now and I hope it's something that the other players feel comfortable with too. I would hate if they felt like they couldn't speak to me about something. It came up over lunch during a camp for an international against Australia when someone was talking about alcohol and Louise Quinn asked how I was dealing with it all. I told her about how I was able to deal with it now, that I can still go out and have a good time but not drink – it's all about mindset. I was glad that Louise asked me.

I think there should be something done in every sporting environment, where the mental aspect is addressed. As a collective, mental health and wellbeing need to come first. Whether it is scoring a winning goal or missing a penalty, sport happens very quickly and how you react in such a short period of time can determine the lasting impact.

As athletes, we always have high expectations and when you don't reach those targets the comedown can be very hard-hitting. If you don't have the right structures in place you dwell on them. That is why a team environment is perfect for dealing with something that can affect the group as a whole. There is no point in ignoring the elephant in the room.

I also appreciate that difficult topics need to be treated carefully; not everyone will want to speak out in a group. But as long as I am playing football I will be willing to share for the betterment of the team. Being part of the Ireland squad means the world to me and I don't ever want something to be a distraction from that.

I guess you learn to value second chances and that is exactly how it is for me today.

Part of my reality now is that my life is completely different to what most athletes would know. There are a lot of things that I need to be cautious about, for example if I take my medication past a certain time it will affect me the next morning and with morning training sessions I can't afford to not be fully on it. I have to be smart with it.

Another really important thing is ensuring that I get the right amount of sleep. If I don't settle down at a certain time then my life turns into a nightmare. This is all part of managing my body, my routine and my life. Without the required amount of sleep, my mind goes into overdrive. Everyone knows what a bad night's sleep does for their mood the next day, but multiply that by 100 and you will begin to understand how bad it can get for me.

Listening to podcasts allows me to steady my focus. One of my favourites is *The High Performance Podcast* which has opened my eyes to other people's points of view and understanding the importance of having a healthy body and mind. I feel that I have developed a good understanding of that but listening to high-performing individuals share their stories allows me to resonate with them and others.

Another really important thing for me is scribbling down my thoughts and feelings in a journal on a regular basis. People wouldn't previously have seen me as someone who writes in a journal, but it is something that I have to do. It calms me, reassures me and allows me to collect my thoughts. Also, it is refreshing to be able to read back through the pages and see how far I have come.

I would like to think now that I have come out of the tail-end of a few horrible experiences. Being in recovery is an amazing experience because it allows you to find out who you truly are. It breaks you down into a million pieces in order to build you back up in a completely different way. Don't get me wrong, there are some really bad days, but it's how I react them and manage them that makes the difference.

Writing this, at this stage in my life, I am happy, content and ready to experience this amazing life that I am grateful for. In a way I'm glad that I was able to go through what I have because it has made me into the person that I am today. You need to grow through what you go through.

I know what I have done in the past and decisions that I have made have really hurt people. With time, I know that I can build that trust back up with people because I'm now sober and will continue to remain sober. I'm excited about what's to come.

13

New Goals

FOOTBALLERS are often quoted as saying that they are taking things game by game. Well, I've adopted that mentality to my life in focusing on the day-by-day routine of it all.

There is no point in thinking too deeply about the future. Instead I stay excited about what might happen and don't take life too seriously.

My recovery is not over yet and probably never will be, so that's something I need to work at every day.

With everything I've been through in my life, I now see things in a completely different way. Of course there are still goals and targets to reach – that will never change – but I measure success in other ways now. For example, completing simple things each day so that I don't slip into a negative headspace is something that I can be proud of.

I've tried to commit suicide twice, but there were many other times that I considered it and that was because I had drifted away from a daily routine. So I cannot ever underestimate the importance of that regularity again.

Something that I really want to continue to work hard at is being a positive role model for others. I'd like to be considered approachable by girls and young women, so that they can learn about my story and maybe relate to it.

That was the sole purpose of doing this book and I hope the sharing of my experiences can help others when they are struggling with their own mental health.

I'm finally comfortable with the tag of being a role model, precisely because of the journey that has led me to this point where I'm in control of my own future. When in hospital, I would dread Monday mornings when the patients had to get up early and make our beds with fresh sheets. Now, I can appreciate a simple task like that as I understand why routine matters.

I've adopted the motto of 'one day at a time'. Every day that I can do the right thing is a successful day and I need to spread that across everything that I do.

Football-wise, I want to keep playing for as long as possible.

I want to keep challenging myself, moving out of my comfort zone and seeing where that leads me. I still have a lot to give for both club and country, so I'm excited about what comes next in that regard.

When I eventually hang up the boots, I would like to work with people who have issues with mental health. While I appreciate that there is some training required to be qualified in that area, I feel that becoming a life coach is a role that I could bring a lot to.

Ultimately, my new goals consist of staying fit, healthy and sober. I have to give myself the best possible chance to succeed at whatever I put my mind to and that will only come by abiding by the lessons I have learned along the way.

Acknowledgements

I WONDER what my former English teacher, Ms Nugent, would think of me now. Never in her wildest imagination could she have foreseen that I would go on to write a book. Yet here we are!

If I'm being honest, I wasn't the most attentive in English class during school, although life has a funny way of taking you down paths that you never would have consciously veered towards before. Writing this book sums up that kind of experience but I'm delighted that I went through with it.

This book would not have been possible without the love and support of my parents, Fiona and Liam, my siblings, Ellen and Philip, my wonderful niece, Emily, and my extended family who have always been there for me with a smile and a hug.

I've put my family through a lot of heartache in the past few years, so this book is my way of acknowledging their unwavering commitment to helping me be healthy and happy.

Many friends have been really important, but especially Amanda Budden, Shannon Dempsey, Danielle Burke and Grace Moloney. They went above and beyond, time and again, whenever I messed up or simply needed a friend to talk to. Without friends like that I'm not sure where I would be.

A huge part of me was shaped by the people in my local community, from the Circle and Broadale, where the different families were always there for me. But Aidan O'Connor, the father of my friend Mark, was and still is a very special influence on my life. He is someone who I can turn to for literally anything.

I owe a special thanks to all of the managers, coaches, medical personnel, support staff, administrators and volunteers who have aided my development as a player, from Douglas Hall, Cork City, Raheny United, Glasgow City and the Republic of Ireland at various age levels.

It would be remiss of me not to thank Laura Montgomery, who has always stood by me. She gave me the opportunity, twice, to play professional football, understood when I fell off the wagon and has always tried to bring out the best in me.

Football is a team sport so I would never have excelled without my team-mates. I've been fortunate enough to play alongside some truly fantastic players but also some amazing people. There are probably too many to mention here, but everyone's helping hand hasn't gone unnoticed.

A big thank you to everyone at Pieta, the drug and alcohol rehabilitation centre in Cork – especially Andrew Fiddow – the various counsellors who have tried to help me and the wonderful staff at Stobhill Hospital.

I'd like to thank Pitch Publishing for taking a chance on me and providing me with a platform to tell my story. And a huge thank you to Gareth Maher, who has been the driver of this project and someone who has been able to transform my scattered thoughts into coherent sentences. It has been quite the journey completing this book.

Career Statistics

Cork City

2011: WNL – 4 games / 1 goal

2012: WNL – 11 games / 4 goals. WNL Cup – 1 game

2017: WNL – 14 games / 12 goals. WNL Cup – 2 games, 3 goals. FAI Cup – 3 games, 3 goals

2018: WNL – 3 games. WNL Cup – 1 game

Total: 39 games, 23 goals

Raheny United

2013: WNL – 6 games, 9 goals. FAI Cup – 3 games, 1 goal

2014: WNL – 4 games, 3 goals. WNL Cup – 3 games. FAI Cup – 1 game

2015: WNL – 2 games. WNL Cup – 1 game

Total: 20 games, 13 goals

Glasgow City

97 games played

67 goals scored

UEFA Women's Champions League

Raheny United – 6 games, 4 goals

Glasgow City – 9 games, 3 goals

Scottish Women's Cup Final

3 appearances (2015, 2016, 2019)

5 goals (3 x 2015, 2 x 2019)

FAI Women's Cup Final

2 appearances (2013, 2017)

1 goal (2017)

Republic of Ireland

26/11/2015: Republic of Ireland 0-3 Spain – UEFA
Women's European Championship Qualifier

02/03/2016: Austria 2-0 Republic of Ireland –
Cyprus Cup

09/03/2016: Republic of Ireland 2-0 Finland –
Cyprus Cup

20/09/2016: Republic of Ireland 0-1 Portugal – UEFA
Women's European Championship Qualifier

08/03/2017: Korea DPR 2-0 Republic of Ireland –
Cyprus Cup

05/03/2020: Republic of Ireland 1-0 Greece – UEFA
Women's European Championship Qualifier

11/03/2020: Montenegro 0-3 Republic of Ireland –
UEFA Women's European Championship Qualifier

Honours

Scottish Women's Premier League: (4) – Glasgow City
2015, 2016, 2019, 2021/22

Scottish Women's Cup: (2) – Glasgow City 2015, 2019

Women's National League: (1) – Raheny United 2013/14

Women's National League Cup: (1) – Raheny United
2014/2015

FAI Women's Cup: (3) – Raheny United 2013, 2014,
Cork City 2017

WNL Team of the Year: (1) – 2017

FAI Women's Under-19 Player of the Year: (1) – 2013

UEFA Women's Under-17 European Championship:
2010 Runner-Up

* These statistics were correct up to the end of
March 2022